THE OFFICIAL
HORIZON
COOKBOOK

THE OFFICIAL

HORIZON

COOKBOOK

TASTES OF THE SEVEN TRIBES

Victoria Rosenthal
and Rick Barba

INSIGHT
EDITIONS

SAN RAFAEL · LOS ANGELES · LONDON

CONTENTS

Ingredients Guide 9
Departure from
  Barren Light 14

UTARU 16
Beanweed Bites 19
Newgrowth Bowls 21
Greenmarrow
  on Wheatslice 23
Wheatslice 25
Spicy Beanweed Morsels 27
Sourfruit Tart 29
Land-God's Libation 33

DESERT TENAKTH 34
Salt Bite Special 37
Feasting Board
  with Haunch 39
Spikestalk Shells 43
Stillsands' Prize 47
The "Off-Duty" 49

SKY TENAKTH 50
Mountain Trail Bread 53
Stuffed Snowbird 55
Land and Lake 57
Charred Greens
  and Grey Omens 59
Mulled Skybrush 61

LOWLAND TENAKTH 62
Lowland Trail Mix 65
Fireclaw Stew 67
Honeyloaf 69
Blood Bread 71
Fruit on Fire 75

OSERAM 76
One-Handed Supper 79
Milduf's Local Stew 81
Bitterbrew Boar 83
Fried Bitter Leaf 85
Meat in the Middle 87
Brew-Battered Wedges 89
Milduf's Treat 91
Sparkale 93

CARJA — 94

Sun Wings	97
Mesa Bread	99
Grazer's Bounty	103
Sun-Seared Ribs	105
Royal Grits	107
Blazed Beans	109
Sunfall Maizemeat	111
Sungria	115

NORA — 116

Valleycakes	119
Forager's Pouch	121
Redthicket Buns	125
Goddess' Gold	129
Crunchleaf Bowl	131
Fens' Fieldbird Stew	133
Matriarch's Joy	135

BANUK — 136

Cured Coldwater Fish	139
Shatterbread	143
Chewcatch	145
Cutfish Cakes	147
Frost-Thaw Soup	149
Blue Light Pudding	151

QUEN — 152

Ruby Sunrise	155
Salty Planks	157
Crab Hot Pot	159
Delta Dumplings	161
Marine's Arrow	165
Ceo's Banquet	167
Imperial Dark Seafoam	171

POTIONS — 172

Health Potion	175
Stamina Potion	177
Cleanse Potion	179
Antidote	181
Overdraw Potion	183
Resist Fire Potion	185
Resist Freeze Potion	187

Conversion Charts	189
Dietary Considerations	190
About the Authors	191

INGREDIENTS GUIDE

Amaretto is a sweet almond liqueur. It has a slightly bitter, almond flavor to it. Amaretto can be substituted with almond extract. Note that almond extract is much more potent and should only be added at one-third the amount.

Ancho chile is a dried poblano pepper with a Scoville scale rating between 1000 and 1500 SHU. It can be replaced with another dried chile of your choice with a similar heat level, but keep in mind that the flavor will be slightly different. Ancho chilies can be stored in a cool pantry.

Areparina flour is a precooked cornmeal. It comes in different varieties, but the kind used for the recipes in this book is the white (blanco) cornmeal. It can be stored in an airtight container in a cool pantry.

Berbere is an Ethiopian spice mixture containing paprika, dried chilies, onion, garlic, fenugreek, and other spices in the makeup of its flavor profile.

Black vinegar is a dark, fermented vinegar made from glutinous rice. It has an acidic, yet slightly sweet, flavor. If needed, you can substitute black vinegar with another rice vinegar. Black vinegar can be stored in a cool pantry.

Bread flour is a high-protein flour, typically containing 12 to 14 percent protein, meant to be used in yeasted breads. The higher protein in the flour helps create more gluten throughout the bread, making it chewier and more elastic.

Bonito flakes, also known as *katsuobushi*, are dried tuna shavings. They are a key ingredient in Japanese cuisine and one of the major components in dashi. Bonito flakes can be used to enhance the flavors of stocks and as a garnish. Store them in a cool pantry.

Caraway seeds are dried fruit of the caraway plant. They have a sharp, nutty, peppery flavor with a hint of licorice (anise). Caraway seeds can be substituted with fennel seeds.

Cardamom is a pod of seeds that can be used either whole or ground. Black cardamom has a smoky, menthol-like flavor great for savory dishes, while the green variety's strong zesty, flowery, earthy flavor is well suited to both savory and sweet dishes. The flavor of cardamom is pretty unique, but a combination of cinnamon, allspice, and nutmeg can serve as a substitute.

Castelvetrano olives are bright green olives grown in Sicily. They have a firm texture and a rich, buttery flavor. These olives can be substituted with another firm green olive.

Cilantro, also known as coriander, includes the fresh leaves and stalks grown from coriander seeds. Cilantro has a citrusy, slightly peppery taste to it. Some people might find that it tastes like soap. Cilantro can be substituted with one-third the amount of parsley.

Fennel is a vegetable and part of the parsley family. It has a mild licorice (anise) flavor and can be consumed raw or cooked. The bulb of the fennel is the typical part used for consumption, and the stalks work well for broths and flavoring. Celery can serve as a substitute.

Fennel seeds are dried seeds from the fennel plant's flowers. They have a sweet, licorice (anise) flavor that pairs well with savory dishes, especially pork. Aniseed can be used as a substitute for fennel seeds, but make sure to use less, because aniseed is much more pungent.

Feta cheese is soft, salty brined cheese made from sheep's milk. It can be easily crumbled because of its soft texture. Cotija cheese can be a substitute for feta.

Fish sauce is a sweet, salty, pungent liquid made from fermented anchovies and salt. The high salt content means fish sauce can be used to replace salt in cases where you want an added layer of umami. Be careful not to use too much, because it can easily overpower a dish. Fish sauce can be stored in the pantry for 2 to 3 years.

Gochujang is a thick Korean chile paste that contains red chile peppers, sticky rice, fermented soybeans, and sweeteners. Heat levels of gochujang vary and are displayed on the container with a spice indicator. Once gochujang is opened, it must be stored in an airtight container in the refrigerator.

Honeycomb is a natural product made by honeybees as the housing used to contain the honey they produce and pollen they collect. It can be stored indefinitely in the pantry in an airtight container.

Horseradish is a sharp, pungent root that can be bought whole, or as a grated product in a jar that should be stored in the refrigerator. It can be substituted with wasabi or mustard powder.

Juniper berries are the small, tart, piney-flavored seed cones of juniper trees. They can be cooked whole or crushed into a fine-ground mixture. Juniper berries pair especially well with wild game meat.

Kalamata olives are dark brown olives originating in Kalamata, Greece. They have a milder taste than black olives and are generally much sweeter and fruitier. Kalamata olives can be substituted with black olives, Niçoise olives, or Gaeta olives.

Kashmiri chile powder is made from dried and ground Kashmiri chilies. The chilies have a mild heat with a vibrant red coloring. Good substitutes for Kashmiri chile powder include paprika and other mild chilies.

Kimchi is a spicy Korean fermented vegetable dish. Napa cabbage is the most common vegetable used for kimchi. It is prepared with a brine and spices, similar to a pickling process, but which also allows the vegetables to ferment. Kimchi must be stored in the refrigerator and occasionally opened to allow pressure from the fermentation to be released.

Kombu is a type of dried kelp used in Japanese cuisine to enhance the flavors of stocks. It can be stored in a cool pantry.

Masa harina is dried corn flour. It can be stored in an airtight container in a cool pantry.

Miso is a paste made from fermented soybeans, often used in Japanese cuisine. It comes in several varieties, including white (the mildest flavor) and red (allowed to age for longer, making it saltier and stronger in flavor). Miso can be stored in an airtight container in the refrigerator.

Negi is a Japanese variety of the Welsh onion. It has a similar taste profile to scallions but is larger, with a longer white stem. Use scallions if you don't have negi available.

Niboshi are dried young sardines. They can be enjoyed as a snack or used for seasoning stocks.

Plantains are related to bananas but are much starchier and can't be eaten raw. Unripe plantains will be green in color. As they ripen, they turn yellow (medium) and eventually black (fully ripe).

Prickly pear is the fruit from the nopal cactus. These fruits can range from green (less sweet) to red (sweeter).

Queso fresco is a fresh, soft Mexican cheese made from cow's milk. The cheese has a salty, mild flavor and can be substituted with a mild feta. Queso fresco should be stored in the refrigerator.

Rye berries are whole rye kernels with the hulls removed and no additional processing done.

Shaoxing wine is a rice wine used in Chinese cuisine. It can be stored in a cool pantry for about 6 months.

Tahini is a paste made from ground white sesame seeds and oil. Store-bought tahini can be stored in the pantry for up to 6 months.

Tomatillo is a tart-flavored fruit wrapped in a papery husk, originating in Mexico. These should not be confused with green tomatoes. Tomatillos, with the husks still on, can be stored in the refrigerator for about 2 weeks.

Vital wheat gluten is wheat flour that has had most of its starch removed, leaving the wheat proteins behind. The protein content is between 75 and 85 percent. Adding it to a dough will yield a chewier and more elastic texture.

Wheat bran is the outer layer of the oat groat. Wheat bran contains a higher amount of fiber and antioxidants. Substitutes for wheat bran include oat bran and rice bran.

Wheat berries are whole wheat kernels with the hulls removed and no additional processing done.

Wild boar meat is a lean, slightly gamy meat. Because these animals are much more active than domesticated pigs, the meat typically cooks quicker than regular pork. Wild boar meat can be substituted with the same cut of pork, but keep in mind that the cook times will be different.

This journal is the property of distinguished cook Milduf Boarbroiler. If found, please help it find its way back to my tavern in Chainscrape. Unless, of course, I bit off more than I could chew, and you've found this beside the "remains" of my perilous misadventure ... In which case ... I guess it's yours now?

DEPARTURE FROM BARREN LIGHT

From atop the wall at Barren Light, I'm watching two Skydrifters circle above a pack of vicious Scrappers, the sunlight glinting off their razor-sharp tails. In the morning, I'll be out there among the untamed wilds of the Forbidden West—some place for a defenseless Oseram cook.

Journeying beyond the safe borders of the Sundom seemed like a great idea a couple of nights ago. I was minding the kitchen at Chainscrape's tavern. An Oseram belly is tough to fill, and that evening a large group of them rolled into town. Gilvarn, a local miner, guzzled down boar stew by my counter and watched as I frantically braised boar and delicately grated fiberzest to feed the newcomers.

I noticed the group's leader headed for my counter, straight as a Charger. My stomach turned. Was I too sparing on the bitter leaf? Were my dough balls too doughy? Not rotund enough? Would he believe my tears were from the fiberzest's noxious yet flavorful mist?

The man stuck out his intimidatingly callused hand in my direction. He introduced himself as Arvund and thanked me. My hearty cooking would be the last square meal his delvers would enjoy for some time, as they were headed into the perilous West. Then, he slid a handful of shards across my counter. Said if I were to join their bold expedition as cook, there'd be much more where that came from.

Overhearing the proposal—and picturing yours truly out in the wilds—Gilvarn snorted so hard stew sprayed out of his nose. I blushed red as a hot kiln. Truth is, the only place I've ever delved is a pantry, and my expertise in the wilds is limited to hearing stories from passing hunters.

Yet at that moment, I thought back to the bravery I had learned months ago when I boldly defied a local gang of ruffians. Something kind of like courage but more like stupidity welled up in me. I loudly proclaimed, so Gilvarn and the rest of the tavern could hear, that I would love to travel into the deadly, machine-infested wilds. Sign me up! Made quite the scene of it, too. You should have seen the faces—mouths agape with shock and concern.

I can't go back to Chainscrape now. I'd never live it down!

    That night, my mind was away with thoughts of the shards I'd earn and a grand dream I never thought could be within my reach: an eatery of my own. I could picture it. Milduf's Forbidden Feeds. Each menu item would be collected on my epic western expedition and unlike anything an Oseram had ever set tongue upon. The queue for tables would run the length of Mainspring.

    And so, after a sleepless night alone in my single bunk, I packed my trusty griddle and joined Arvund's crew on the trek to Barren Light.

    In you, Journal, I'll collect recipes and document my travels. But for now, I should go. This Carja border guard has been eyeing me. Apparently, "the wall is for security purposes only." He says that I'm "distracting the guards" and insists that "I don't need to read everything I am writing out loud."

    I'll show him, though. Months from now, he'll be the one finding himself on the very long wait list at Milduf's in Meridian!

UTARU

— PLAINSONG —

I'm starting to think "Forbidden West" isn't clear enough of a name. Why not the Forsaken West? Deadly West? Or the Really-Actually-Don't-Come-Here-It's-For-Your-Own-Good West?

Sure, Arvund's guys have taken care of the machines so far (barely). But I can't help feeling like a Glinthawk's about to swoop in and make minced Milduf with every creak of the caravan's wheels. Honestly, would it be so hard for these delvers to oil their axles?!

Likely death aside, the sights are as breathtaking as they are terrifying. Yesterday, we walked beneath the rusted tentacles of a long-dead Metal Devil. Arvund repeated whispers that the Savior of Meridian defeated one such machine in far-off lands. Hoping to curry favor with the group, I casually mentioned that I'd met the Savior—she'd even procured a temporary griddle for yours truly!

Arvund laughed and suggested I focus on cooking up meals, not fantasies. With that attitude, I hope he likes his boar stewed a minute too long!

Rather than stooping to the level of his snide comment, I turned my attention to the region's confounding ruins. Each looked like an enormous serving bowl, standing high off the ground on iron legs. How large were the creatures that the Old Ones fed from these?

Our first destination, the Utaru capital, Plainsong, was built atop three of these great dishes and appeared like a humungous green salad on the horizon.

I couldn't picture a less Oseram place! Sure, there wasn't a forge, smeltshop, or masonry in sight, but it was a marvel to behold. Rather than iron and stone, the buildings

are woven intricately from light wood and enshrined in lush foliage—a truly breathtaking fire hazard!

   The crew and I ascended its wooden walkways and separated to stock up for the road ahead. After a few confused loops—and stumbling into a grumpy band of rehearsing musicians called "the Chorus"—I found my way to the local cook, Daen.

   Daen answered my many questions about Utaru food. He explained the tribe's crops are provided mainly by a herd of docile Plowhorns they call land-gods. Because of this, many Utaru are free to spend their days focusing on weaving, crafting, and in Daen's case, cooking.

   His food was strange yet delightful. Rather than eating from individual plates, Daen, his kin, and I sat around a single large platter. Edge to edge, it was loaded with Wheatslice, Spicy Beanweed Morsels, and Beanweed Bites. We picked the plate clean like Scrappers over a bounty of salvage. This felt like truly sharing a meal.

   Unfortunately, I returned to find the crew wasn't as open-minded or open-stomached as I was. They grumbled about the Utaru's leaf-filled diet, insisting they would not eat like squirrels the whole trip. Guess I could see their point, as we all audibly suffered from our bean-heavy dinners well into the night.

   Yet, with this first stop behind us, I'm feeling confident that this expedition might not be so bad.

BEANWEED BITES

I haven't been long in the Forbidden West, yet my culinary horizons are already widening. Turns out, you don't need meat to create a hearty dish so long as you've carefully balanced your seasoning and have a solid stock of beanweed. Even some of Arvund's carnivores were appreciative of these luscious bites. Or so I gathered from their chorus of burps.

DIFFICULTY: ◆ ◆ ◇ ◇ ◇

PREP TIME: 15 minutes   **COOK TIME:** 30 minutes   **YIELD:** 4 servings   **DIETARY NOTES:** Vegan, Alcohol

BEANWEED BITES
¼ cup cornstarch
2 teaspoons kosher salt
½ teaspoon ground black pepper
16 ounces firm tofu, cut into bite-size pieces
Canola oil, for the pan
2 garlic cloves, chopped

SAUCE
2 tablespoons soy sauce
1 tablespoon Shaoxing wine
1 teaspoon rice vinegar
1 teaspoon ground cinnamon
½ teaspoon ground fennel
½ teaspoon ground star anise
1 teaspoon ground black pepper

1. Combine the cornstarch, salt, and pepper in a medium bowl. Add the tofu and toss to coat. Combine all the ingredients for the sauce in a small bowl.

2. Heat a medium pan with 1 teaspoon of canola oil over medium-high heat. Add the tofu and cook until all sides have slightly browned, about 3 to 5 minutes per side. Transfer to a plate.

3. Add more oil and the garlic and cook until golden brown, about 2 to 4 minutes.

4. Add the sauce and tofu and cook until the tofu is coated and the sauce has been absorbed, about 3 minutes.

NEWGROWTH BOWLS

In recent, difficult times, the leaf-loving Utaru resorted to eating meat in the form of a dish unappetizingly named "Oldgrowth Gruel." They've since returned to their plant-filled diets, but many had grown to enjoy the dish. So, Daen developed this meat-free alternative. Having not tasted the former, I can only say this version is a delight.

DIFFICULTY: ◆◆◇◇◇

PREP TIME: 45 minutes **INACTIVE TIME:** 8 hours **COOK TIME:** 1 hour
YIELD: 4 to 6 servings **DIETARY NOTES:** Vegetarian, Dairy-Free, Gluten-Free

- ⅓ cup plus 1 tablespoon dried adzuki beans
- ⅓ cup plus 1 tablespoon glutinous rice
- 2 tablespoons walnuts, crushed
- 4 cups water
- One ½-inch piece ginger, julienned
- 2 tablespoons honey
- 2 tablespoons sugar
- 2 teaspoons kosher salt

1. Place the adzuki beans in a large bowl with enough water to just cover them. Cover with a kitchen towel and let soak for 6 hours.

2. When the 6 hours are up, add the rice and walnuts to the bowl and soak for another 2 hours.

3. Bring a medium pot with 4 cups of water to a boil over medium-high heat. Strain the beans, rice, and walnuts.

4. Once the water has come to a boil, add the beans, rice, and walnuts to the pot. Give it a few stirs and bring to a boil again. Once boiling, stir once more, reduce the heat to low, cover, and let cook for 40 to 50 minutes, until all the ingredients have softened.

5. Add the ginger, honey, sugar, and salt and whisk together. Taste and season with additional salt and sugar if needed.

NOTE: This dish goes really well with a soft-boiled or poached egg on top!

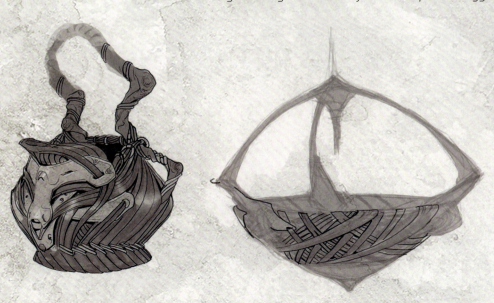

GREENMARROW ON WHEATSLICE

Some cooks, especially in eateries frequented by snooty Carja noble types, think good recipes need to be complicated and precisely assembled. Wrong. I think the simpler, the better—it gets my customers fed faster. This honey-drizzled leafeater's dish proves just that. It's best served on Wheatslice, which I'll also jot down the recipe for.

DIFFICULTY: ◆◇◇◇◇

PREP TIME: 10 minutes **YIELD:** 1 salad **DIETARY NOTES:** Vegetarian, Dairy-Free

½ avocado
1 thick slice Wheatslice (page 25), as is or toasted to preference
1 tablespoon honey
3 to 4 small slices honeycomb
1 radish, sliced
Kosher salt, to taste
Ground black pepper, to taste

1. Place the avocado in a bowl and lightly mash until it reaches the desired consistency.

2. Transfer onto the wheatslice and spread into an even layer. Drizzle with honey and top with a few small slices of honeycomb. Season with salt and pepper. Finally, top with the radish.

WHEATSLICE

Making good bread can be trickier than wrangling a disturbed Burrower, but this Utaru recipe is nearly as foolproof as it is delicious. The aroma of Wheatslice loaves baking in the kiln is like inhaling a whiff of good cheer. With every bite, I swore I could hear the harmonic hum of Utaru voices.

DIFFICULTY: ◆◆◆◇◇

PREP TIME: 30 minutes **INACTIVE TIME:** 24 hours **COOK TIME:** 50 minutes
YIELD: 1 loaf **DIETARY NOTES:** Vegetarian, Dairy-Free

2½ cups whole wheat flour
1½ cups bread flour, plus more for the counter
1 tablespoon kosher salt
2 teaspoons active dry yeast
2¼ cups warm water
¼ cup honey

EQUIPMENT
Dutch oven

1. Combine the flours, salt, and yeast in a large bowl. Combine the warm water and honey in a small bowl and whisk until the honey dissolves.

2. Pour the honey water into the large bowl and mix until the dough just comes together. It will be extremely sticky at this point.

3. Cover the bowl and let rise at room temperature for 1 hour. Transfer to the refrigerator and let rise for 18 to 24 hours.

4. Take the dough out of the refrigerator and generously flour a working surface and your hands with bread flour. Remove the dough from the bowl, lightly knead, and shape into a round ball. Place on a piece of parchment paper and cover with a kitchen towel for 1 hour.

5. Preheat the oven to 425°F. Place an empty Dutch oven with a lid in the oven to preheat for 30 minutes. Once the dough has risen, cut an X across the top of the loaf.

6. Transfer the dough with the parchment paper into the preheated Dutch oven. Cover with the lid and bake for 35 minutes. Remove the lid and bake for another 10 to 15 minutes, or until the loaf is done. Place on a wire rack to cool completely before cutting.

SPICY BEANWEED MORSELS

Beanweed, beanweed, beanweed. The Utaru eat the stuff constantly. That puts pressure on their cook to find ingenious methods to bring new life to this staple. Daen uses a deep brown fermented condiment, along with some more common seasonings, to bring a bit of fire to this forest. I hope this dish will draw sweat from the brows of many Oseram in the future.

DIFFICULTY: ◆◆◇◇◇

PREP TIME: 1 hour **INACTIVE TIME:** 24 hours **COOK TIME:** 20 minutes **YIELD:** 4 servings **DIETARY NOTES:** Vegan

PICKLED VEGETABLES
½ cup water
½ cup rice vinegar
1 tablespoon apple cider vinegar
1 tablespoon maple syrup
Pinch of kosher salt
½ cucumber, thinly sliced
½ daikon, thinly sliced
½ carrot, thinly sliced

SPICY BEANWEED MORSELS
16 ounces firm tofu, cut into bite-size pieces
¼ cup gochujang
½ cup soy sauce
2 tablespoons maple syrup
1 tablespoon rice vinegar
1 teaspoon sesame oil
1 teaspoon potato starch
Canola oil, for the pan
6 shiitake mushrooms, sliced
6 ounces baby bok choy, cut into bite-size pieces
3 scallions, chopped

FOR ASSEMBLY
2 cups cooked rice
4 ounces kimchi, chopped

TO MAKE THE PICKLED VEGETABLES:
1. Combine the water, rice vinegar, apple cider vinegar, maple syrup, and salt in a large airtight container. Add the cucumber, daikon, and carrot. Cover and place in the refrigerator for at least 24 hours. Can be stored in the refrigerator for about 1½ weeks.

TO MAKE THE SPICY BEANWEED MORSELS:
2. Place the tofu on a plate, top with another plate, and set a heavy object (such as a cast-iron skillet or a few food cans) on top. Allow to sit for 10 minutes in order to press out excess liquid. In a large bowl, combine the gochujang, soy sauce, maple syrup, rice vinegar, sesame oil, and potato starch. Whisk together until smooth. Add the tofu, cover, and let marinate in the refrigerator for 1 hour.

3. Heat a large pan with 1 teaspoon of canola oil over medium-high heat. Strain the tofu in a mesh strainer to remove excess marinade, reserving at least ¼ cup of the marinade.

4. Add the tofu to the pan and cook until all sides have slightly browned, about 2 to 3 minutes per side. Transfer to a plate.

5. Add more canola oil to the pan, along with the shiitake mushrooms and bok choy. Cook until the vegetables have softened, about 5 to 8 minutes. Add the scallions and cook for another 3 minutes.

6. Add the tofu and reserved sauce. Cook until the sauce has been absorbed, about 3 minutes.

7. Serve with cooked rice, kimchi, and the pickled vegetables.

SOURFRUIT TART

These berry pastries offer a sweet yet sour flavor unlike anything in the Claim. I imagine I'll prep these beforehand and put them on display in my eatery's window so the bright colors will draw people in. I could see these becoming quite popular with the provincial, inner-Mainspring types.

DIFFICULTY: ◆◆◆◆◆

PREP TIME: 1 hour **INACTIVE TIME:** 8 hours **COOK TIME:** 25 minutes
YIELD: 12 tarts **DIETARY NOTES:** Vegetarian, Alcohol

PASTRY CREAM

6 egg yolks
½ cup sugar
Juice and zest of 1 lime
1 teaspoon kosher salt
¼ cup cornstarch
2 cups coconut milk
1 vanilla bean, split open and seeds scraped
2 cardamom pods, crushed

TO MAKE THE PASTRY CREAM:

1. Combine the egg yolks, 2 tablespoons sugar, lime juice and zest, salt, and cornstarch in a medium bowl and set aside. Whisk together the remaining sugar, the coconut milk, vanilla bean and seeds, and cardamom pods in a medium saucepan. Heat on medium-high until right before the mixture starts to boil. Reduce the heat to low.

2. Scoop out ½ cup of the mixture and slowly transfer to the bowl with the egg yolks while whisking. Repeat twice.

3. Slowly add the yolk mixture back into the saucepan. Increase the heat to medium-low and whisk everything together until it thickens.

NOTE: *This step should take about 10 minutes. You'll get a workout, but it'll eventually come together.*

4. Once the base has thickened, remove from the heat. Remove and discard the vanilla bean pod and cardamom pods. Pour the pastry cream into an airtight container and allow to cool to room temperature.

5. Cover and let chill in the refrigerator for 8 hours. The pastry cream can be stored there for up to 3 days.

TART SHELLS

1 cup plus 3 tablespoons all-purpose flour
½ cup almond flour
½ cup powdered sugar
½ teaspoon kosher salt
½ cup unsalted butter, cubed and chilled
2 egg yolks
1 teaspoon vanilla paste
1 tablespoon coconut milk

GLAZE

½ cup apricot jam
1 tablespoon lemon juice
2 tablespoons amaretto

FOR ASSEMBLY

12 tart shells
24 ounces berries, any variety

EQUIPMENT

4-inch tart tins
Pie weights

TO MAKE THE TART SHELLS:

6. Combine the flours, powdered sugar, and salt in a food processor. Add the cubed butter. Pulse until the mixture resembles coarse meal with a few chunks of butter.

7. Add the egg yolks, vanilla paste, and coconut milk. Pulse until the dough comes together. Remove the dough from the food processor and lightly knead to bring it all together. Split into two portions, wrap each in plastic wrap, and place in the refrigerator for at least 1 hour.

8. Take one of the dough portions and split it into four pieces. Roll one of the pieces out to the size of a 4-inch tart tin. Carefully lay the dough in the tin and remove any excess. Prick the bottom of the tart with a fork and place on a large baking sheet. Repeat with the remaining dough pieces. Place the baking sheet with the tarts in the freezer for 10 minutes before baking.

NOTE: *If you only have a few small tart tins, you can do the preparation and baking steps in smaller batches. Just make sure to leave any unused dough in the refrigerator until your tins are completely cooled and ready to use again.*

9. Preheat the oven to 375°F. Place a small piece of parchment paper on top of each of the crusts. Fill with pie weights (or dry beans) to help keep the crusts from rising. Bake for 10 minutes.

10. Take the tarts out of the oven and remove the parchment paper and weights. Return to the oven and bake until the crusts are golden brown, about 3 to 5 minutes. Allow the tarts to cool slightly before removing from the tins and setting on a wire rack to cool completely.

TO MAKE THE GLAZE:

11. Place all the glaze ingredients in a small saucepan. Heat over medium-high heat and whisk until combined. Remove from the heat and set aside.

TO ASSEMBLE:

12. Place the pastry cream in the tarts, smoothing the surface so it lines up with the top of the crust.

NOTE: *Only assemble these tarts if you plan to consume them the same day. The cream and glaze will soak into the crusts over time and make them soggy.*

13. Top with a variety of berries to your liking. Carefully brush the glaze on top of the fruit to give them a nice shine. The tarts can be stored in the refrigerator for up to 8 hours.

LAND-GOD'S LIBATION

This beverage brings together the sweetest produce the Utaru lands have to offer. It's traditionally enjoyed at seasonal festivals, where they raise a mugful in honor of their land-gods for providing a fruitful harvest. The flower blossoms are prized by the Utaru, and I can taste why. They may be difficult to cultivate in the Claim, but I'll do what I can to re-create this refreshing concoction!

DIFFICULTY: ◆◇◇◇◇

PREP TIME: 30 minutes **INACTIVE TIME:** 8 hours **COOK TIME:** 30 minutes
YIELD: 2 smoothies **DIETARY NOTES:** Vegetarian, Dairy-Free

ELDERFLOWER SYRUP
¾ cup honey
2 limes, sliced
½ cup water
1 tablespoon elderflower blossoms

SMOOTHIES
6 ounces spinach
1 frozen banana
½ cup frozen mango
¼ ripe avocado
1 cup coconut milk
2 tablespoons elderflower syrup

EQUIPMENT
Blender

TO MAKE THE ELDERFLOWER SYRUP:
1. Whisk together the honey, limes, and water in a small saucepan and place over medium-high heat. Once the honey dissolves, add the elderflower blossoms and bring to a simmer. Remove from the heat, cover, and let steep for 10 minutes.

2. Strain into an airtight container. Allow to cool to room temperature. Store in the refrigerator for at least 8 hours before serving. Can keep for up to 2 weeks. This recipe makes enough syrup for about 16 smoothies.

TO MAKE THE SMOOTHIES:
3. Place everything in a blender. Blend until smooth. Split between two large glasses.

DESERT TENAKTH

— SALT BITE —

The first signs of trouble appeared at the High Turning. We passed between this border crossing's lofty walls to find them abandoned, scorched, and pierced with bolts from some recent battle. I was sure a straggler hid above, waiting for a chance to make Oseram skewers with their fire arrows.

We made it through unambushed but then found ourselves in the harsh Tenakth desert. The dry grass cracked like burnt pastry under our boots. Even simple ingredients like beanstem and paleberry were scarce. And Arvund's order that we avoid areas populated by locals made hunting difficult.

As a cook, I've had too few hands, too few griddles, and occasionally been a little low on an ingredient. But now, I had the lousy job of rationing. I wasn't looking forward to invoking the wrath of the short-fused delvers. So, when I heard the early morning honks of geese, I concocted a genius—and less confrontational—solution. SMASHED EGGFRY!

While the crew slept, I snuck out. I easily gathered a bounty of eggs, sustaining minimal injuries from my skirmish with a razor-beaked mother goose. But as I descended victoriously from the nest, I found a Tenakth patrol waiting, weapons drawn.

I dropped the eggs and fell to my knees. My pleas only frustrated their leader, Chatakka, who clicked his fingers at a soldier. "Gag the thief before he attracts machines."

I was led by spear-point to a village that looked as ferocious as my captors. Its wood buildings came together in sharp points, offering plenty of opportunities for my impalement. I wondered why they'd give such a terrifying place a name as appetizing as Salt Bite.

From my cage, I overheard soldiers debate punishments. Some favored of abandoning me among the dunes. One saw value in keeping me around…as machine bait. Another suggested my tear ducts would make for a steady water source. And they wouldn't even hear out any of my own suggestions!

Finally, Chatakka stepped in. As my captor, the final decision was his—I'd fight for my freedom in their Melee Pit. "It would surely be entertaining," he laughed.

I contemplated my doom as the sun set. But as the cold night arrived, so did *she*.

Pentalla. Her hair was fashioned into two delicate fins like carp playing in a stream. She wore a frown that could light up a room, and her dark face paint brought out her captivating gravy-brown eyes, which glistened in the torch fire.

She placed a bowl of food by my cage and removed my gag. Too entranced by her presence to summon a proper greeting, I immediately took a fragrant, crispy morsel from the bowl and shoved it into my mouth. At first, the flavor was outstanding. Then, I felt the heat build. First, on my tongue, then in my eyes. I stayed composed for the most part, though my gasps for breath may have given me away.

"Apologies," Pentalla remarked, "my apprentice may have over-spiced the Lizard Bites. Not unexpected from her. Unsuitable for what may be a final meal. But it'll have to do."

I tried to reply but only produced jumbled noises. Just as Pentalla turned to leave, I managed to tame my wounded tongue. "Bidder leaf! Do balance oud ledthorn bebber!"

She turned. "Bitter Leaf? Hmph. Might be worth trying."

I seized the opportunity to explain that I, too, am a cook. I hadn't knowingly stolen. I was here to collect recipes, exchange knowledge, and learn from cooks as skilled as herself. She responded with a mysterious silence. Then, she disappeared into the night.

In the morning, I was awoken by a firm yet sweet kick to my ribs.

"Wake up. We are leaving."

Wiping the sandy drool from my face, I saw Pentalla standing over me. "You are spared the Pit for now, cook. It cost a month's worth of Salted Haunch, but seeing your punishment through now rests upon me."

Through a mouthful of haunch, Chatakka called out, "Good luck out there, you two!" as we departed.

SALT BITE SPECIAL

Though the Desert Clan may be known for its strength, this dish requires a surprisingly delicate touch. The bird-based innards are straightforward enough to prepare, but shaping the perfect egg pouch to fold around these fillings takes mastery. Thankfully, Pentalla is as skilled with a spatula as with a blade. When sourcing ingredients for this dish, it's best to ensure you are far from any Tenakth patrols.

DIFFICULTY: ◆◆◆◇◇

PREP TIME: 30 minutes **COOK TIME:** 45 minutes **YIELD:** 4 servings **DIETARY NOTES:** Dairy-Free, Gluten-Free

FILLING

1 chicken breast
2 garlic cloves, crushed
1 stalk lemongrass
½ lemon, sliced
1 bay leaf
½ teaspoon kosher salt
½ ounce chicken bouillon
2 tablespoons olive oil
1 red bell pepper, sliced
½ onion, sliced
1 teaspoon chili powder
1 teaspoon ground cumin
½ teaspoon garlic powder
½ teaspoon ground coriander

FOR ASSEMBLY (PER SERVING)

3 eggs, beaten
¼ of the filling

TO MAKE THE FILLING:

1. Place the chicken breast, garlic, lemongrass, lemon, bay leaf, salt, and chicken bouillon in a small pot. Fill with water until the chicken is covered and bring to a boil over medium-high heat. Lower heat to low and allow to simmer for 10 to 15 minutes, until the chicken registers an internal temperature of 165°F. Remove the chicken from the water and let cool. Once the chicken has cooled enough to handle, shred it by hand and set aside.

2. Preheat a large nonstick pan over medium-high heat. Add the olive oil and allow to heat. Add the bell pepper and onion and sauté until softened, about 8 to 10 minutes. Season with the chili powder, cumin, garlic powder, and coriander. Toss to coat and continue to sauté until the onion turns golden, about 8 to 10 more minutes.

3. Add the shredded chicken to the vegetables and toss to coat. Heat until the chicken is warmed up. Remove from the heat and set aside until the omelet is ready.

TO ASSEMBLE:

4. Begin warming a medium pan over medium heat. Spray with nonstick spray. Once it is warmed, add the beaten eggs and give a few good swirls with a spatula. Spread out and let cook for about 3 minutes, or until the edges begin to solidify. Carefully flip the omelet and allow to cook for another minute. Remove from the pan and carefully transfer onto a plate.

5. Scoop a hearty portion of the filling over half of the omelet. Fold the other half on top to cover the filling slightly.

FEASTING BOARD WITH HAUNCH

As it's the food Pentalla bartered for my freedom, haunch will always be close to my heart. Dried in the desert heat for months, this cured meat is a long-lasting provision highly valued among the Tenakth. Even when served, it is rationed sparingly. It's shaved into ribbon-like slivers and served on a platter with various flavorsome pastes. When these components meet on a soft flatbread, you can begin to understand why it was a worthwhile trade!

DIFFICULTY: ◆◆◇◇◇

PREP TIME: 1 hour **INACTIVE TIME:** 3 hours **COOK TIME:** 1 hour **YIELD:** 6 to 8 servings **DIETARY NOTES:** N/A

HUMMUS
One 15.5-ounce can chickpeas, drained and rinsed
¼ cup tahini
2 garlic cloves
3 tablespoons lemon juice
3 tablespoons water
2 tablespoons olive oil
1 teaspoon kosher salt

BABA GHANOUSH
2 eggplants
½ cup olive oil, plus more for serving
4 garlic cloves
⅓ cup tahini
½ teaspoon ground cumin
1 teaspoon kosher salt
2 tablespoons lemon juice

TO MAKE THE HUMMUS:
1. Place all of the hummus ingredients in a food processor. Pulse until the mixture is smooth. If the mixture is too thick to mix, add an extra teaspoon of water at a time. Transfer to an airtight container and store in the refrigerator. Can be stored for up to 1 week.

TO MAKE THE BABA GHANOUSH:
2. Preheat the oven to 350°F. Poke several holes in each of the eggplants and rub with olive oil. Place on a baking tray and bake for 1 hour, or until softened. Let cool, remove and discard the skin, and roughly chop into big cubes.

3. Transfer the eggplant into a food processor with the garlic, tahini, cumin, and salt. Pulse until the mixture is smooth.

4. Slowly stream in the ½ cup of olive oil and lemon juice while pulsing the food processor to combine. Transfer to an airtight container and let refrigerate for at least 3 hours before serving.

HAYDARI

3 tablespoons unsalted butter
2 garlic cloves, chopped
1 tablespoon dried mint
5 ounces feta cheese
2½ cups plain yogurt
2 tablespoons fresh dill, chopped

FOR ASSEMBLY

¼ cup kalamata olives
¼ cup Castelvetrano green olives
¼ cup pimento-stuffed olives
1 cup artichoke hearts
10 figs, cut in half
20 mini tomatoes
2 cucumbers, sliced
10 radishes, sliced
6 ounces prosciutto
5 ounces feta cheese, cubed
5 whole pockets pita bread, quartered

TO MAKE THE HAYDARI:

5. Heat a small nonstick pan with the butter over medium-high heat. Once the butter has melted, add the garlic. Cook until golden, about 2 to 3 minutes. Add the dried mint and remove from the heat. Allow to cool completely.

6. Smash the feta cheese in a medium bowl. Add the yogurt and mix until well combined. Add the melted butter mixture and dill. Mix until well combined. Transfer to an airtight container and store in the refrigerator. Can be stored for up to 1 week.

TO ASSEMBLE:

7. Prepare the hummus, baba ghanoush, and haydari in separate bowls. Arrange on a large serving tray adorned with the other ingredients.

SPIKESTALK SHELLS

The true measure of a cook is how they can work with the limited ingredients their territory offers. This recipe can use either a paddle of spikestalk (thorns removed, of course) or its fruit. These are grilled, then placed into soft shells, and finished with a mix of refreshing toppings and a luscious sauce. Interestingly, Tenakth diners will often assemble their own shell's-worth of ingredients, customizing the flavors to their personal tastes.

DIFFICULTY: ◆◆◆◇◇

PREP TIME: 45 minutes   COOK TIME: 45 minutes   YIELD: 4 servings   DIETARY NOTES: Vegetarian

CREAMY TOMATILLO SALSA

2 tomatillos, husks removed and cut in half
1 garlic clove
1 serrano pepper
1 poblano pepper, cut in half and seeds removed
½ bunch cilantro
2 scallions
Juice of 1 lime
½ teaspoon kosher salt
1 teaspoon ground black pepper
½ cup sour cream

TO MAKE THE CREAMY TOMATILLO SALSA:

1. Preheat the oven broiler. Place the tomatillos, garlic, and both peppers on a baking sheet. Put the baking sheet under the broiler and cook until the tomatillos have charred slightly, about 5 minutes. Flip everything and place back under the broiler. Cook until the other side has slightly charred, about 5 more minutes.

2. Remove from the oven and allow to cool. Transfer to a food processor. Add the cilantro, scallions, lime juice, salt, and pepper. Pulse the food processor until smooth. Add the sour cream and pulse until just combined. Season with additional salt and pepper if needed. Can be stored in an airtight container in the refrigerator for up to 1 week.

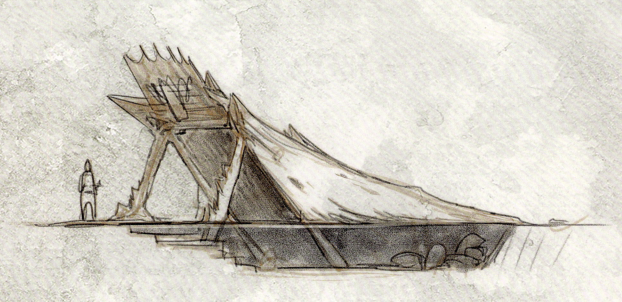

NOPALES

12 ounces nopales, chopped (make sure all the spikes are removed before cooking)

1 tablespoon canola oil

½ onion, chopped

1 jalapeño pepper, chopped

2 teaspoons chili powder

2 teaspoons ground cumin

1 teaspoon ground coriander

1 teaspoon Mexican oregano

2 tablespoons adobo sauce

¼ cup water

Kosher salt, to taste

Ground black pepper, to taste

½ bunch cilantro

FOR ASSEMBLY

Tortillas

Avocado

Cilantro

Queso fresco

TO MAKE THE NOPALES:

3. Place the nopales in a mesh strainer and rinse them. Bring a medium-size pot of water to a boil. Add a generous pinch of salt to the pot. Add the nopales and simmer for 20 minutes.

4. Drain with a mesh strainer and rinse the nopales again. Heat a medium-size nonstick pan with the canola oil over medium-high heat. Add the nopales and heat until all of the liquid has evaporated and the nopales have become golden, about 10 minutes.

NOTE: *The liquid that the nopales exude is very slimy. It is extremely important to remove as much liquid as possible to eliminate that texture.*

5. Add the onion and jalapeño and sauté until all softened, about 10 minutes. Add the chili powder, cumin, coriander, Mexican oregano, adobo sauce, and water. Cook for another 5 minutes, until all of the water has evaporated. Season with additional salt and pepper.

6. Remove from the heat and add the cilantro.

TO ASSEMBLE:

7. To assemble the tacos, simply warm some tortillas up and spread a generous amount of creamy tomatillo salsa. Top with avocado, cilantro, nopales, and queso fresco.

STILLSANDS' PRIZE

The heat of the Stillsands is brutal. But at night, especially on the bordering cliffs, the temperature plummets. Pentalla developed this ingenious concoction while on tedious night watch shifts as a young soldier. She would often bring the juice of spikestalk fruit with her, and she noticed it would freeze in the cold. She then began to use these icy nights to prepare a frozen treat that—if properly stored—could be enjoyed as a reprieve from the daytime heat.

DIFFICULTY: ◆◇◇◇◇

PREP TIME: 30 minutes **INACTIVE TIME:** 12 hours **YIELD:** 5 popsicles **DIETARY NOTES:** Vegan, Gluten-Free

1 cup prickly pear cactus water
¼ cup lime juice
¾ cup coconut milk
2 tablespoons sugar

EQUIPMENT
Popsicle molds
Popsicle sticks

1. Add all ingredients to a medium bowl and whisk until well combined.
2. Transfer the mixture into popsicle molds. Insert the popsicle sticks, cover, and place in the freezer for at least 12 hours, ideally overnight.

THE "OFF-DUTY"

The life of a Desert Tenakth soldier is arduous. And so, after a long day patrolling sands and battling machines, many will unwind with this juice. Prepared with alcohol distilled from spikestalks, this drink bites like a Slitherfang (or so I would imagine). Just one put yours truly right to bed.

DIFFICULTY: ◆◇◇◇◇

PREP TIME: 10 minutes   **YIELD:** 2 drinks   **DIETARY NOTES:** Vegan, Gluten-Free, Dairy-Free, Alcohol

1 sprig mint, plus more for serving
Ice, plus more for serving
4 ounces prickly pear cactus water
½ ounce simple syrup
1 ounce lime juice
2 ounces tequila
Lime wedges, for serving
3 ounces club soda

EQUIPMENT
Cocktail shaker

1. Muddle the mint in a cocktail shaker. Add the ice, prickly pear cactus water, simple syrup, lime juice, and tequila. Cover and shake for 10 seconds.
2. Prepare 2 glasses with fresh mint, a lime wedge, and ice. Split the shaken cocktail between the glasses and top with club soda.

SKY TENAKTH

— STONE CREST —

Apparently, we're heading to the "Memorial Grove," and there, Pentalla will request "a more fitting punishment," whatever that is. I don't know what to make of her—if she'd hoped for my painful demise, she wouldn't have saved my skin, as she has done many times on the road.

We weren't long on the road before a Watcher attacked us. What's great about Pentalla is she knows when I yell, "Please! No!" I really mean, "Drive your spear into the soft bit between its plating, then gut it like a fish." We're like hammer and tongs: I keep the machine occupied, and she whacks it.

Thankfully, we took down the Watcher before it could alert its friends—a machine convoy blocking our path. Bristlebacks. Behemoths. Leaplashers. You name it.

Like any great cook, Pentalla kept her cool when the kitchen got hot. She had a plan. "If Runner's Wild is impassable, we'll take the path through Stone Crest."

It'd take more nights, but that was fine with me. More time 'til my day in Tenakth court and more time getting to know Pentalla—for her recipes, of course.

Unfortunately, it turns out Stone Crest is kind of cold. And high up. And where an Oseram would build a handy bridge over a cavernous break in a mountain path, the Tenakth balance along a wooden beam like some Carja circus act. No, thank you!

Pentalla had crossed so easily, and I didn't want her to think I couldn't. So I went for it. My first step was okay. So was the second. But on the third, I looked down. A goat below caught my eye, and I couldn't help noticing it looked the size of an insect. I lost my nerve and hugged the log beneath me. By this point, several impolite Sky Tenakth told me to get going or get falling. Eventually, we all agreed it'd be best to tie a rope 'round my belly and reel me in like a prize fish!

The night was setting in when we entered the small settlement pitched up along the mountain path. We paid a visit to the cook, who refused to prepare a meal for "an outlander and some scorpion from the Desert Clan." I was dreading the thought of sleeping hungry after such an arduous day. But then, Pentalla pulled a pure white snowbird from her pack. "A shame. The outlander caught this. We'd hoped you could help us prepare it, but it seems you've buried your head too far up your Bulwark."

"*He* hunted this?" The cook's eyes widened. He let out a defeated sigh, placing several pots atop his fire. "We can make this work." He began to prepare the Stuffed Snowbird, and his cold disposition melted like goat butter. He explained how rare this dish was. I'd likely be the second foreigner to taste it—ever!

He shared multiple recipes as we ate beside an unnecessarily precarious overlook. I know people say Tenakth are hard to get along with. In fact, I get the feeling they don't really like each other that much. But it seems like if you can get past their hard exterior, and you make them not want to kill you, and you're a defenseless prisoner, and you give them food, they're pretty okay.

Later on, as we lay full-bellied in our bedrolls, I asked Pentalla when she'd caught the snowbird.

"I shot it while you snored through the night. Next time you produce such a racket, I may put sandbugs up your nose. Take care of the blockage for you."

She wants to take care of it for me, Journal! And, I've been promised a wood-beam-less route down to the Lowlands!

Things are looking up. But for now, sleep.

MOUNTAIN TRAIL BREAD

Though the highlands around Stone Crest are cold, rugged, and somewhat terrifying, the local bread is as warm and comforting as any I've ever sampled. Chopped nuts and dried fruits give it a rich, pleasing texture, and I'm particularly fond of its subtle yet sharp spices. If you must make camp on a precipitous edge of doom, you want this bread in your travel pouch.

DIFFICULTY: ◆◆◆◇◇

PREP TIME: 45 minutes **INACTIVE TIME:** 8 hours **COOK TIME:** 1 hour
YIELD: 1 loaf **DIETARY NOTES:** Vegetarian, Dairy-Free

3 cups all-purpose flour
½ cup bread flour
2 teaspoons kosher salt
1 teaspoon ground cardamom
1 teaspoon ground cinnamon
1 tablespoon sugar
2 teaspoons active dry yeast
¼ cup dried cherries
⅓ cup dried cranberries
½ cup golden raisins
½ cup walnuts, chopped
½ cup pecans, chopped
1½ cups warm water
Olive oil, for brushing

EQUIPMENT
Dutch oven

1. Combine the flours, salt, cardamom, cinnamon, sugar, yeast, dried fruit, and nuts in a large bowl. Pour the water into the bowl and mix together until the dough just comes together. If it is too sticky, add more all-purpose flour. Lightly knead for 3 minutes.

2. Brush a bowl with olive oil and place the dough inside. Brush the top of the dough with more olive oil. Cover and let the dough rise at room temperature for 8 hours.

3. Remove the dough from the bowl, lightly knead, and shape into a round ball. Place on a piece of parchment paper and cover with a kitchen towel for 1 hour.

4. Preheat the oven to 425°F. Place an empty Dutch oven with a lid in the oven to preheat for 30 minutes. Once the dough has risen, cut three slashes in the top of the loaf.

5. Transfer the dough with the parchment paper into the preheated Dutch oven. Cover with the lid and bake for 30 minutes. Remove the lid and bake for another 20 to 30 minutes, or until the loaf is done. Set on a wire rack to cool completely before cutting.

STUFFED SNOWBIRD

After completing a death-defying ritual known as "The March of the Ten," victorious Sky Tenakth will often be asked if they want their celebratory Snowbird stuffed or encrusted. This special Sky Tenakth delicacy is well worth the hassle of collecting its rare ingredients. The bird is filled with a rich stuffing of browned omens, fried sausage, cheese, herbs, and jam. Each bite is a sampling of the mountains' most delicious offerings.

DIFFICULTY: ◆◆◆◆◇

PREP TIME: 1 hour **INACTIVE TIME:** 30 minutes **COOK TIME:** 1 hour **YIELD:** 6 quails **DIETARY NOTES:** Alcohol

1 onion, chopped
¾ pound venison sausage, removed from casing
1 king oyster mushroom
½ teaspoon kosher salt
¼ cup white wine
¼ cup parsley, chopped
½ cup panko
2 ounces goat cheese
¼ cup fig jam
6 semi-boneless quail
Olive oil, for brushing
Kosher salt, to taste
Ground black pepper, to taste

1. Preheat a medium nonstick pan over medium-high heat and spray with nonstick spray. Add the onion and sauté until softened, about 5 to 8 minutes.

2. Add the sausage and cook until browned, about 5 minutes. Add the mushroom and cook until any liquid is evaporated and the mushroom is golden brown, about 10 to 12 minutes. Season with salt.

3. Pour in the white wine to deglaze the pan. Cook until all the wine has evaporated, about 2 to 3 minutes, then transfer to a large bowl. Add the parsley, panko, goat cheese, and fig jam and mix until well combined. Taste and season with additional salt if needed. Set aside and allow to cool completely.

4. Prepare a large baking sheet with aluminum foil topped with a sheet of parchment paper.

5. Take one of the quail and scoop about ½ cup of the filling into the cavity. Secure by piercing a toothpick through both legs and into the lower part of the quail. This will help keep the legs upright during the cooking process. Transfer to the prepared baking sheet, breast side up. Repeat this step with the remaining quail.

NOTE: *Make sure not to overstuff the quail. Try to keep them evenly filled to ensure that all six will cook evenly.*

6. Place the baking sheet in the refrigerator and let the quail rest for 30 minutes.

7. Preheat the oven to 400°F. Remove the baking sheet from the refrigerator. Brush each quail with olive oil and season with salt and pepper. Bake in the oven for 30 minutes, or until the quail is cooked through.

8. Turn on the broiler and allow the skin to turn golden brown, about 3 to 5 minutes.

55

LAND AND LAKE

Coldwater fish caught in a chilly, clean mountain stream is some of the freshest eating I've ever enjoyed. The Sky Clan's domain fortunately has an abundance of such waterways. When our host introduced us to this particular recipe, Pentalla couldn't help but give an approving nod. Perhaps I could improvise a fishing net and surprise her with this dish in the coming days.

DIFFICULTY: ◆◆◆◇◇

PREP TIME: 30 minutes **COOK TIME:** 40 minutes **YIELD:** 2 servings **DIETARY NOTES:** Dairy-Free, Gluten-Free

Two 8-ounce whole rainbow trout, guts removed and cleaned
Olive oil, for coating
Kosher salt, to taste
Ground black pepper, to taste
8 slices lemon
8 sprigs thyme
4 sprigs parsley
4 slices thin bacon

1. Preheat the oven to 425°F. Rub each of the rainbow trout with olive oil, inside and out. Season with salt and pepper. Cut 4 of the lemon slices in half and place 4 half slices inside each trout. Stuff each trout with half of the thyme and parsley, then top each with 2 slices of lemon. Wrap each trout with 2 slices of bacon, making sure to cover the lemon so it is held in place.

2. Preheat a large cast-iron skillet over medium-high heat and coat with olive oil. Once heated, add the rainbow trout non-lemon side down. Heat until the bacon on the bottom crisps up, about 5 minutes.

3. Transfer to the oven and bake for another 20 to 25 minutes, until the fish is cooked through. Turn on the broiler to crisp up the bacon on top, about 3 to 5 minutes. Remove from the oven and let sit in the skillet for 5 minutes before serving.

CHARRED GREENS AND GREY OMENS

One thing we Oseram share with the Tenakth: We can't help but blacken everything we see. Even vegetables are not spared the fire. This easy-to-make Sky Clan recipe chars tender greens together with the mountain's plentiful grey omens to create a simple yet succulent side dish—perfect on a plate with Stuffed Snowbird!

DIFFICULTY: ◆◇◇◇◇

PREP TIME: 15 minutes **COOK TIME:** 25 minutes **YIELD:** 4 to 6 servings **DIETARY NOTES:** Vegan, Gluten-Free

- 14 ounces broccolini, cut into 3-inch pieces
- 10 ounces oyster mushrooms, cut into 3-inch pieces
- 2 tablespoons olive oil
- ½ teaspoon kosher salt
- ¼ teaspoon ground black pepper

1. Preheat the oven to 425°F. Place the broccolini, oyster mushrooms, and olive oil in a large bowl. Toss until well coated.

2. Line a large baking tray with aluminum foil and top with a sheet of parchment paper. Transfer the oiled vegetables to the tray, spreading into an even layer. Season with salt and pepper and bake in the oven for 20 to 25 minutes, or until the vegetables are crispy.

MULLED SKYBRUSH

Living in the frigid Sheerside Mountains is, to put it mildly, uncomfortable. Even moreso in the winter months. To stave off the cold, many Sky Tenakth will warm themselves with this spiced, sweetened, and heated wine. As one drinks it, one can feel the cold falling away, at least for a moment.

DIFFICULTY: ◆◇◇◇◇

PREP TIME: 10 minutes   COOK TIME: 15 minutes   YIELD: 4 servings
DIETARY NOTES: Vegan, Gluten-Free, Alcohol

1 blood orange, sliced
1 lemon, sliced
3 mandarin oranges, sliced
3.5 ounces blueberries
6 whole cloves
2 cinnamon sticks
3 whole star anise
One 750-milliliter (25-ounce) bottle blueberry wine
1½ cups cranberry juice
¼ cup amaretto
⅓ cup maple syrup

1. Combine all the ingredients in a large pot. Place over medium heat and bring to a low simmer for 15 minutes. Serve hot.

LOWLAND TENAKTH

— THE MEMORIAL GROVE —

I didn't know air could be so wet. We've been in the Lowlands a few days, and I'm so sticky you could roll me in wheatcrumb, throw me in some hot kindleweed oil, and serve deep-fried Milduf. Not to mention, the trees on the way down had it in for me. If I never hear the words "slide rope" again, I'll die happy.

Speaking of my possible demise, we arrived at the Memorial Grove. It appears to be like any other overgrown ruin ripe for delving. But the treasures inside—the "Visions"—aren't the kind you can plunder. Seeing the Old Ones as great statues chiseled from light, I realized how similar we really were (but were they really so tall?!). My astonishment was cut short by Pentalla sending me to wait outside during my trial. "Tenakth don't respect the meek. This shouldn't take long. Be safe. I won't make a habit of saving your neck."

I would've pointed out there's a difference between meek and cautious, were I not overjoyed at Pentalla's apparent concern for my well-being. But there was no time to dwell on either. The roar of a distant crowd drew me to the mouth of an Arena, where many market stalls stood empty—I figured every Tenakth and their commander must be inside the Arena itself, cheering at some great spectacle.

As I wandered, I caught the scent of simmering jungle bird. My nose led me to a preoccupied cook. "If you're hungry, outlander, order now." A great explosion sounded from the Arena, followed by another cheer. "Soon, I will be overrun. This crowd is always ravenous." The cook snapped at his assistant, "Keep stirring that Fireclaw Stew."

I asked why he doesn't feed the crowd while they're in the Arena, avoiding the rush—I'm an Oseram, and we'll eat pretty much anywhere, anytime. "Hot stew in an unruly crowd?" he laughed. "That's asking for trouble."

This gave me a thought that carried me to the cook's spare countertop. I began to make dough. "If I weren't preoccupied, I'd remove your hands for touching my wares," the cook quipped, "and you'll pay for those ingredients."

In no time, I had a platter of Meat in the Middle ready to go. I headed for the Arena. The atmosphere inside was unlike anything I'd felt before. As hunters battled deadly machines below, the crowd's energy shook the building like a pot threatening to boil over.

I made my way past rows of seats, swapping shards for servings. When I returned to the stall empty-plattered, the cook noted my success. He, too, began to knead dough, then snapped at his assistant, "Why are you wasting time stirring?! Help the Oseram!"

Together, we hawked round after round of my meaty pastries, and when the Arena finally emptied, it was not with a violent stampede but a lethargic dawdle. The cook slapped my back with joy and invited me to sit. "Some dish, outlander. It's only fair I teach you mine in return."

I happily sat, scribbled, and learned. In my excitement, it slipped my mind that nearby, my fate was being decided. When I noticed night had fallen, I bolted back to the Grove, where Pentalla sat on the foundations of a ruined wall, sharpening an intimidating pile of arrows. I approached timidly and asked, "Are those…for my punishment?"

"Which one? For your theft? Or for leaving me to sit like stew?" She looked up as I awkwardly cowered. A smile crossed her face. "I have been named Ration Improvement Envoy. In exchange for your freedom, you will guide me through the eastern tribal lands as I collect intel on meal preparation techniques."

I fell to my knees and thanked her. No machine baiting! No melee pits! And I get to go home!

"Seems the Marshals were in a good mood. They'd come from the Arena. Some foreigner had stuffed the spectators with so much food there was hardly any post-match brawling."

I promised to teach her to make Meat in the Middle at our next stop.

LOWLAND TRAIL MIX

This mix of nuts and dried fruits is a standard ration for Tenakth deployed into the sprawling, dense jungles of the Raintrace. Expeditions can be long and unpredictable—it's not uncommon for even experienced Lowlanders to become lost among the machine-infested, maze-like woods. This salty and sweet morsel can last as long as its carrier can resist eating it.

DIFFICULTY: ◆◇◇◇◇

PREP TIME: 15 minutes **COOK TIME:** 10 minutes **YIELD:** 10 servings **DIETARY NOTES:** Vegetarian

½ cup macadamia nuts
1 cup cashews
¾ cup almonds
⅓ cup banana chips
¼ cup dried mango, sliced
¼ cup dried ginger, sliced
¼ cup dried pineapple, chopped
⅓ cup dried jackfruit, sliced
¼ cup dark chocolate chips
¼ cup coconut flakes

1. Preheat the oven to 350°F. Place the macadamia nuts, cashews, and almonds on a baking sheet lined with parchment paper. Bake for 8 to 10 minutes, or until the nuts are lightly toasted. Set aside to cool completely.

2. Once cooled, combine everything together in an airtight container. Shake to mix well. Can be stored in an airtight container at room temperature for up to 1 week.

FIRECLAW STEW

This is the fiery recipe my Lowland acquaintance was broiling outside the Arena before I came to his aid. Pentalla was skeptical about whether the spice would hold up to her Desert Clan tongue, but when I whipped up a batch, she was pleasantly surprised. Various meats can work, but I prefer the ground mutton of the very first serving I tasted.

DIFFICULTY: ◆◆◇◇◇

PREP TIME: 45 minutes **COOK TIME:** 4 hours **YIELD:** 4 servings **DIETARY NOTES:** Dairy-Free, Gluten-Free

2 teaspoons kosher salt
1 teaspoon ground black pepper
2 tablespoons ground cumin
2 tablespoons spicy chili powder
1 tablespoon ground coriander
1 tablespoon paprika
1 teaspoon ground cinnamon
½ tablespoon cocoa powder
1 tablespoon dark brown sugar
Olive oil, for the pot
2 pounds ground lamb
2 onions, chopped
6 garlic cloves, chopped
1 jalapeño pepper, chopped
1 poblano pepper, chopped
2 serrano peppers, chopped
One 6-ounce can tomato paste
One 28-ounce can diced tomatoes
2 bay leaves

1. Combine the salt, pepper, cumin, chili powder, coriander, paprika, cinnamon, cocoa powder, and dark brown sugar in a bowl.

2. Place a deep pot with olive oil over medium-high heat. Add the lamb and cook until it has all browned. Add the spice mixture and mix until well combined. Transfer to a plate.

3. Add more olive oil if needed, then sauté the onions until soft, about 8 minutes. Add the garlic and cook for another minute. Add the peppers and cook until softened, about 5 minutes.

4. Stir in the browned lamb, tomato paste, and diced tomatoes. Bring to a simmer. Finally, add the bay leaves, cover, and lower the heat to low. Simmer for 4 hours, making sure to stir once every hour or so. Once cooked, remove and discard the bay leaves.

HONEYLOAF

Fresh from the oven and slathered with butter, Honeyloaf is the perfect complement to Fireclaw Stew. It has a sweet aroma and its crumbly texture soaks up gravies and thick sauces, ensuring that none of the flavors on a customer's plate will go to waste. Not to mention, it's quick to prepare. With this kind of versatility, it will undoubtedly serve as a hearty accompaniment for many of the dishes at Milduf's.

DIFFICULTY: ◆◆◇◇◇

PREP TIME: 15 minutes **COOK TIME:** 25 minutes **YIELD:** 10 servings **DIETARY NOTES:** Vegetarian

1 cup cornmeal
1 cup all-purpose flour
¼ cup light brown sugar
1 tablespoon baking powder
2 teaspoons kosher salt
½ cup unsalted butter, melted and cooled, plus more for the skillet
2 tablespoons olive oil
¼ cup maple syrup
2 tablespoons honey
2 eggs
1¼ cups coconut milk
1 tablespoon lime juice

1. Preheat the oven to 425°F. Prepare a cast-iron skillet by rubbing it with butter.

2. Combine the cornmeal, all-purpose flour, light brown sugar, baking powder, and salt in a large bowl. Whisk together the melted butter, olive oil, maple syrup, honey, eggs, coconut milk, and lime juice in a small bowl. Pour the wet mixture into the large bowl. Mix until just combined.

3. Transfer to the prepared cast-iron skillet. Bake for 20 to 25 minutes. Allow to cool before cutting to serve.

BLOOD BREAD

I had to ignore the grisly name and focus instead on the astonishing innovation of this flatbread dish. When boiled, fried, and broiled, the fruit takes on a pulled-swine-like texture, while a zesty spice mix and sugar provide a meaty flavor. In jest, the Tenakth refer to this topping as "Utaru Boar." The assembly is fun, too—hammering dough will be a great way to work out those frustrations from rude customers!

DIFFICULTY: ◆◆◆◆◇

PREP TIME: 1 hour   **INACTIVE TIME:** 24 hours   **COOK TIME:** 40 minutes   **YIELD:** 3 pizzas   **DIETARY NOTES:** Vegetarian

PIZZA DOUGH

- 2½ cups bread flour, plus more for the counter
- 1 tablespoon vital wheat gluten
- 1 teaspoon active dry yeast
- 2 teaspoons sugar
- 1 teaspoon kosher salt
- 1½ teaspoons garlic powder
- ½ teaspoon onion powder
- 1¼ cups water
- 2 tablespoons olive oil

TO MAKE THE PIZZA DOUGH:

1. The day before you plan to make the pizza, prepare the dough. Place the flour, vital wheat gluten, yeast, sugar, salt, garlic powder, and onion powder in the bowl of a stand mixer. In a small bowl, combine the water and olive oil. Pour the liquid into the bowl of the stand mixer.

2. Place the bowl in the stand mixer with a dough hook attachment, and mix on low until all the ingredients come together. When the dough forms into a ball, increase the speed to medium and knead for 5 minutes.

3. Lightly flour your countertop and place the kneaded dough, then smooth it into a ball. Spray a large bowl with nonstick spray (or rub with olive oil), set the dough ball in the bowl, and cover the bowl with plastic wrap. Place in the refrigerator for at least 24 hours, no more than 48 hours.

4. The next day, remove the dough from the refrigerator at least 30 minutes before you start to prepare your pizza. Punch the dough down and place onto a lightly floured countertop. Split into three portions and form into balls. Cover with a clean towel and let rest for ½ hour.

BBQ JACKFRUIT

One 20-ounce can young green jackfruit in water
1 tablespoon light brown sugar
1 teaspoon paprika
2 teaspoons chili powder
1 teaspoon garlic powder
1 teaspoon ginger powder
1 teaspoon kosher salt
½ teaspoon ground black pepper
1 tablespoon canola oil
¾ cup vegetable broth
½ cup barbecue sauce

FOR ASSEMBLY

Olive oil, for the skillet
¼ cup pineapple, sliced
¼ red onion, sliced
Cornmeal, for the skillet
One 13-ounce jar pizza sauce
24 ounces mozzarella, shredded

TO MAKE THE BBQ JACKFRUIT:

5. Drain the jackfruit with a mesh strainer. Rinse a few times and set aside to dry for 10 minutes. Combine the brown sugar, paprika, chili powder, garlic powder, ginger powder, salt, and ground pepper in a medium bowl. Add the jackfruit and toss to coat.

6. Heat a medium nonstick pan with the canola oil over medium-high heat. Add the seasoned jackfruit and sauté for 5 minutes. Add the vegetable broth and bring to a simmer. Reduce the heat to medium and cover. Simmer until the broth has evaporated, about 15 minutes.

7. Uncover and increase the heat back to medium-high. Add the barbecue sauce, toss to cook, and heat until warmed up, about 3 minutes. Remove from the heat and set aside until you are ready to assemble the pizzas.

TO ASSEMBLE:

8. Preheat the oven to 475°F. Heat a medium nonstick pan with olive oil over medium-high heat. Add the pineapple and sauté until golden brown, about 5 minutes. Transfer to a plate and set aside. Return the pan to the heat and add more olive oil. Add the red onion and sauté until softened and golden brown, about 8 to 10 minutes. Transfer to a plate and set aside.

9. Prepare a cast-iron skillet by rubbing the bottom and sides thoroughly with olive oil and then sprinkling generously with cornmeal. Lightly flour a countertop and pound one of the dough portions into a disk shape, continuing to stretch it until slightly wider than the cast-iron skillet. Transfer the dough into the skillet.

10. Top the dough with pizza sauce, then with one-third each of the mozzarella, BBQ jackfruit, pineapple, and red onion. Brush the crust on the edge with additional olive oil. Place on the stovetop over medium-high heat and cook until the bottom of the dough begins to turn brown, about 5 minutes.

11. Transfer the cast-iron skillet to the oven and bake until the cheese is melted and the crust is lightly browned, about 10 to 12 minutes.

12. Repeat Steps 9 to 11 for the remaining two dough portions.

FRUIT ON FIRE

Combining the scorching heat of the desert, ice of the mountains, and fresh fruits of the Lowlands, this treat celebrates the unity of the Tenakth tribe, though it was once only a Lowland specialty. The cook told me to "cook the cherries until they look like the thick blood of an enemy." While that image isn't particularly appetizing, the syrup itself has a fresh, savory essence.

DIFFICULTY: ◆◆◇◇◇

PREP TIME: 30 minutes **INACTIVE TIME:** 24 hours **COOK TIME:** 20 minutes
YIELD: 4 servings **DIETARY NOTES:** Vegan, Alcohol

COCONUT WHIPPED CREAM
One 13-ounce can coconut cream
⅓ cup powdered sugar
Pinch of kosher salt

COOKED CHERRIES
1 pound cherries, pitted
¼ cup light brown sugar
2 tablespoons palm sugar, chopped
1 tablespoon lemon juice
¼ cup cherry liqueur
1 scoop nondairy ice cream, per serving (optional)

TO MAKE THE COCONUT WHIPPED CREAM:

1. Place the can of coconut cream in the refrigerator and let rest for 24 hours. This is done to separate the coconut cream from the coconut water.

2. Open the can of coconut cream and transfer the thick, white cream to a medium bowl. Whip with a hand mixer for 30 seconds to loosen it a bit.

3. Add the powdered sugar and salt. Whip until fluffy, about 3 minutes. Immediately use the coconut whipped cream as garnish for the cherries.

TO MAKE THE COOKED CHERRIES:

4. In a tall saucepan, combine the cherries, light brown sugar, palm sugar, and lemon juice. Place over medium-high heat and bring to a simmer. Simmer until the sugars have fully dissolved.

5. Remove from the heat source and add the cherry liqueur. Mix together well.

NOTE: *It is important to be safe when cooking with alcohol. Always remove from the heat source before adding alcohol to a pan or pot, to avoid spilling any on the burners.*

6. Return to the heat and bring back to a simmer. Cook for 10 minutes, or until the liquid has reduced by half and the alcohol has cooked off. Keep an eye on the mixture as it cooks, because the liquid will bubble up.

7. Prepare a bowl with a scoop of nondairy ice cream, and top with the cooked cherries and the coconut whipped cream.

OSERAM

— CHAINSCRAPE —

Traveling with an Envoy is great! We got personal escorts through the Shining Wastes. And you better believe those soldiers were well fed with two cooks on the trail. As we went, Pentalla taught me dozens of uses for spikestalk. Turns out just 'cause something's thorny doesn't mean it's not sweet inside.

Part of me was sad seeing the wide plains of the West disappear as we were safely enveloped by the Daunt's high cliffs. Though it felt smaller than ever, seeing Chainscrape lit a fire in my oven—the smell of molten iron and the sweet sawdust on the breeze.

As we entered the tavern, a bleary-eyed worker hugged me harder than necessary. "Milduf! You're back! If I'm looking a might thin, it's 'cause your assistant couldn't fill your apron."

Chainscrape's heart is the tavern, and the kitchen's great fire is what keeps it pumping. Pentalla admired its many-layered grill. "You could cook meat for ten squads with a single fire."

She then watched with a mix of curious wonder and skeptical judgment while I prepared a platter of my greatest hits: a perfect mingling of salt, lard, and fire that makes for a classic Oseram feed. As I was showing off where the fat drippings are collected, my regular heckler Gilvarn called over from his table. "Ah, the great adventurer returns!" he hiccupped. "Didn't last long out there, did ya?"

I ignored the gibe and hoped Pentalla hadn't heard. But Gilvarn stood and raised his pint high. "Everybody! To the brave explorer Milduf and his lady captor!" Gilvarn's table, a group of workers a few ingredients short of a dish, all erupted with laughter.

Pentalla reached for her spear, but I gestured for her to stop. I whispered that I knew just how to deal with guys like this. We would over-boil their riverbloom by a minute or two. Get the leaves real chewy. That'd show 'em.

Pentalla rolled her eyes and, without hesitation, threw a peeling knife toward Gilvarn's group. The blade

skewered a fried fowl leg to the wood of their table. "And where have you and your torpid band journeyed in the cook's absence?" she called. "From the ale tap to the shrubs outside and back again?"

The other tables around broke out in a nervous chortle. Another miner, this one more thuggish, stood and reached for his hammer. "I ain't come here to listen to some painted-up barbarian."

Pentalla took a step toward him. "Then perhaps we need to see about removing those troublesome ears." The thug was short but broad and swung his hammer up over his shoulder, knocking over jugs of forgefroth as he stepped into my former kitchen.

Pentalla met his approach, towering head and shoulders over him.

I reached around for something, anything, to help from afar. I settled on a modestly sized baby potato. If I threw the vegetable, it would certainly create enough of a distraction to get us out of there and maybe even leave a nasty bruise that would inconvenience the thug for days to come!

"Steep your coals! Both of you!" Petra's voice rang through the tavern. She'd been a fair-handed leader to Chainscrape since Ulvund was ousted. "If you can't play nice, you'll have to leave." Relief washed over me. "That means you, too, Milduf. Sorry. Your friend's a little blade-happy."

I said we were getting our food for the trail. We have a very important cable car to catch. The fresh air makes for a nicer dining hall than this smoked-out shack, anyway.

We ate as we walked to the cable car. I can still hear Pentalla's words as I write this. "You're a good cook. But you're shaky as a prairie dog in a sandstorm." Pentalla took a bite of Forge-Blackened Sirloin. "And what's with the vegetable?"

I looked down to find the baby potato still gripped in my hand.

ONE-HANDED SUPPER

There's no hunger like that of an Oseram worker. I wanted to create a whole dinner they could carry with them. That's when it came to me—a bowl made from bread so you could eat that, too! I filled it with all kinds of cheeses and threw a hearty egg on top, and BAM! One-Handed Supper.

DIFFICULTY: ◆◆◆◆◇

PREP TIME: 1 hour **INACTIVE TIME:** 2 hours **COOK TIME:** 20 minutes **YIELD:** 2 khachapuris **DIETARY NOTES:** Vegetarian

DOUGH
- ¾ cup warm water (no hotter than 110°F)
- 2 teaspoons active dry yeast
- 2 teaspoons sugar
- 1 tablespoon olive oil
- 1 cup all-purpose flour, plus extra for kneading
- ¾ cup bread flour
- ½ tablespoon garlic powder
- 1 teaspoon kosher salt
- 1 to 2 tablespoons of milk, if needed

FILLING
- 8 ounces mozzarella, shredded
- 4 ounces goat cheese
- 8 ounces feta cheese

TOPPING
- 2 eggs
- 2 tablespoons unsalted butter, divided
- Parsley, chopped, for garnish

1. Combine the water, yeast, sugar, and olive oil in a large bowl. Allow to rest for 5 minutes. Add the flours, garlic powder, and salt. Mix until the dough just comes together. Transfer to a lightly floured work surface and knead for 10 to 15 minutes. If the dough is too sticky, add 1 tablespoon of flour at a time. If it is too dry, add 1 tablespoon of milk at a time.

2. Smooth the dough into a ball. Spray a large bowl with nonstick spray (or rub with olive oil). Place the dough ball into the bowl and cover with plastic wrap. Place in a warm spot and let rest until it doubles in size, about 2 hours.

3. Line two small baking sheets with parchment paper. Once the dough has risen, take it out of the bowl and punch down. Split into two equal portions. Place one back in the bowl.

4. Take the other half and roll out into a 12-inch-long oval. Roll the bottom edge up about 2 inches. Repeat with the top to form two walls with a large center. Pinch the two ends together—the dough should be roughly football-shaped at this point. Transfer to one of the prepared baking sheets. Repeat with the other portion.

5. Cover with a kitchen towel and let rise for 30 minutes.

6. While the dough rests, preheat the oven to 475°F. Combine all of the cheeses for the filling. Remove the kitchen towel from the prepared doughs. Carefully split the cheese mixture between the two doughs.

NOTE: *Do not press on the sides of the dough; you want the dough to keep its height. Also, this might seem like a lot of cheese, but make sure you use it all.*

7. Once the oven is preheated, place the khachapuri inside and bake for 10 to 12 minutes, or until the cheese has melted and the dough has roughly browned. Remove from the oven and make a small divot in the cheese. Carefully crack an egg into each divot.

8. Return to the oven and cook until the egg sets, about 8 to 10 minutes. Once cooked through, top each khachapuri with 1 tablespoon of butter and a sprinkling of parsley.

MILDUF'S LOCAL STEW

I know these Oseram recipes like the oil burns on the back of my hands. I invented half of them! But it never hurts to record one's knowledge for posterity. The Savior herself praised this stew, I'm proud to say. When Aloy sampled her first bowl—after helpfully sourcing a grooved griddle for me from an upriver Scrounger pile—she called it "inspired." You could barely taste the machine oil!

DIFFICULTY: ◆ ◆ ◇ ◇ ◇

PREP TIME: 1 hour   **INACTIVE TIME:** 12 hours   **COOK TIME:** 5 hours   **YIELD:** 4 servings   **DIETARY NOTES:** Dairy-Free, Alcohol

MARINATED WILD BOAR

- 1½ pounds wild boar, cut into large chunks
- 2 thyme stalks
- 1 rosemary stalk
- 3 garlic cloves, crushed
- 1 tablespoon juniper berries
- 2 cups red wine

STEW

- ½ cup all-purpose flour
- 1½ teaspoons kosher salt
- 1½ teaspoons ground black pepper
- 2 teaspoons ground sage
- ½ teaspoon ground cloves
- Marinated wild boar
- Canola oil, for the Dutch oven
- 2 onions, thinly sliced
- 2 red onions, thinly sliced
- ⅓ cup light brown sugar
- 6 garlic cloves, minced
- 3 carrots, cut into bite-size pieces
- 1½ cups beef stock
- 2 tablespoons cornstarch
- 2 cups Trappist ale
- 2 bay leaves
- ½ pound Yukon Gold potatoes, peeled and cut into bite-size pieces

EQUIPMENT

Dutch oven

TO MAKE THE MARINATED WILD BOAR:

1. Place the wild boar, thyme, rosemary, garlic cloves, and juniper berries in an airtight container. Add just enough wine to cover everything. Cover and shake to mix together. Refrigerate for at least 12 hours (or overnight) to help pull some of the gamy flavor from the meat.

2. The next day, drain off the marinade through a fine-mesh strainer. Rinse the meat in cold water to remove excess wine. Remove the wild boar from the spices and thoroughly pat dry. Discard everything but the boar meat.

TO MAKE THE STEW:

3. In a large airtight bag, combine the flour, salt, pepper, ground sage, and ground cloves. Add the wild boar, shake to coat, and transfer to a plate.

4. Heat a medium Dutch oven over medium-high heat and add 1 tablespoon of canola oil. Add a single layer of the wild boar, being careful not to overcrowd the pan. Brown all sides of the meat, about 5 to 8 minutes. Remove and place on a plate. Add more canola oil, if needed, and continue this process until all the wild boar has been browned.

5. Add the onions and additional canola oil if needed. Sauté the onions until caramelized, about 20 minutes. Add the brown sugar and garlic. Cook for 2 minutes, or until fragrant.

6. Preheat the oven to 300°F. Return the wild boar and any juices to the Dutch oven, add the carrots, and stir everything together. Combine the beef stock and cornstarch in a bowl and whisk until smooth. Add to the Dutch oven and stir together.

7. Add the Trappist ale to the Dutch oven and stir together. Finally, add the bay leaves. Cover, place in the oven, and cook for 3 hours, or until the meat is tender.

NOTE: *Make sure to check and lightly stir the stew every 45 minutes while it cooks.*

8. Add the Yukon potatoes and cook for another 30 minutes, or until the potatoes are soft. Uncover the Dutch oven and cook for another 20 minutes.

BITTERBREW BOAR

The thing that makes this boar recipe stand out is the 24-hour airtight wine soak. This helps deliver perfect texture with less gamey flavor. After marinating the leg, I always give it a thorough rub with my savory spice mix for additional seasoning. It's a surefire hit—the hardest part is making friends with a Carja to source good wine.

DIFFICULTY: ◆ ◆ ◇ ◇ ◇

PREP TIME: 1 hour   INACTIVE TIME: 30 hours   COOK TIME: 4½ hours
YIELD: 6 servings   DIETARY NOTES: Dairy-Free, Gluten-Free, Alcohol

MARINATED WILD BOAR

4 pounds wild boar bone-in leg
One 750-milliliter (25-ounce) bottle red wine
1 cup water
5 garlic cloves, smashed
3 bay leaves
2 tablespoons black peppercorns
2 sprigs rosemary
2 sprigs thyme

ROAST

Olive oil, for coating
¼ cup light brown sugar
1½ tablespoons kosher salt
1 tablespoon garlic powder
1 tablespoon ground fennel
1 tablespoon onion powder
2 teaspoons ground black pepper
2 teaspoons ground fenugreek
1 teaspoon ground cumin
2 fennel bulbs, quartered
2 carrots, quartered
2 onions, quartered
2 parsnips, quartered
4 celery stalks, quartered

TO MAKE THE MARINADE:

1. Combine all of the marinade ingredients in an airtight container. Refrigerate for at least 24 hours.

2. Reserve 1 cup of the marinade and place in the refrigerator until needed. Remove the leg from the marinade, discard the rest, and pat the leg dry. Place on a baking sheet with a wire rack. Rub the leg with olive oil.

3. Combine the brown sugar, salt, garlic powder, ground fennel, onion powder, black pepper, fenugreek, and cumin in a small bowl. Rub the boar leg with the spice mixture, covering everything. Place in the refrigerator, uncovered, and let rest for 4 hours.

TO MAKE THE ROAST:

4. Preheat the oven to 275°F. Remove the boar leg from the refrigerator 30 minutes prior to baking. Fill the bottom of a deep baking dish with the fennel bulbs, carrots, onions, parsnips, celery, and the reserved cup of marinade. Set the leg on top of the vegetables and bake in the oven until the meat reaches an internal temperature of 150°F, about 3 to 4 hours.

5. Remove the baking dish from the oven and loosely cover with aluminum foil. Increase the oven temperature to 500°F. Let the baking dish sit until the oven is ready, then remove the aluminum foil and place back in the oven. Cook until the boar leg crisps up, about 4 to 5 minutes. Flip the leg and bake until the other side is crisp, about 4 to 5 minutes. Remove from the oven and cover again in aluminum foil. Let rest for 30 minutes before cutting to serve.

83

FRIED BITTER LEAF

Now, greens are rarely the way to an Oseram's heart, but this dish is the exception. In my humble opinion, the best way to serve greens is fried up with diced swine and fowl stock. This way, the leaves soak up all those tasty, fatty juices. Fried Bitter Leaf's great as a side for Bitterbrew Boar or as a quick, hearty snack.

DIFFICULTY: ◆◆◇◇◇

PREP TIME: 15 minutes **COOK TIME:** 40 minutes **YIELD:** 6 servings **DIETARY NOTES:** Gluten-Free

16 ounces collard greens, stems removed and chopped
1 tablespoon canola oil
4 slices bacon, chopped
6 garlic cloves, minced
1 chicken bouillon cube
Kosher salt, to taste
Ground black pepper, to taste

1. Add the collard greens to a large pot and cover with water. Place over medium-high heat and simmer for 30 minutes. Drain and set aside.

2. Heat a large nonstick pan with the canola oil over medium-high heat. Add the bacon and cook until cooked through and slightly crispy, about 6 to 8 minutes. Add the garlic and cook until softened, about 2 minutes. Crumble the chicken bouillon and mix until completely dissolved. Add the boiled collard greens and panfry until the greens are covered with the garlic and chicken bouillon flavoring. Taste and season with salt and pepper.

MEAT IN THE MIDDLE

This is the first dish a plucky young Milduf ever came up with and probably my signature creation. Delvers and hunting parties will line up down the road for these logs of minced and seasoned mutton wrapped in crisp pastry. It's the kind of meal everyone can agree on, hence the rather ingenious name.

DIFFICULTY: ◆◆◆◇◇

PREP TIME: 30 minutes   INACTIVE TIME: 45 minutes   COOK TIME: 45 minutes   YIELD: 8 servings   DIETARY NOTES: N/A

FILLING

- 3 garlic cloves, minced
- 2 shallots, minced
- 1 tablespoon olive oil
- 1 pound ground lamb
- 1 tablespoon fresh mint, chopped
- 1 tablespoon ground fennel seeds
- 2 teaspoons dried thyme
- 1 teaspoon dried oregano
- 1 teaspoon ground black pepper
- 1 teaspoon kosher salt
- 1 teaspoon Worcestershire sauce
- 2 tablespoons panko

FOR ASSEMBLY

- 1 sheet puff pastry, defrosted
- 1 egg
- 1 teaspoon water
- 1 teaspoon white sesame seeds
- 1 teaspoon black sesame seeds
- 1 teaspoon dehydrated onion flakes

TO MAKE THE FILLING:

1. Heat a frying pan with nonstick spray over medium-high heat. Add the garlic and shallots and sauté until softened, about 5 minutes. Add the olive oil and allow to heat for a minute.

2. Transfer to a bowl and allow to cool completely. Add the ground lamb, fresh mint, fennel seeds, thyme, oregano, black pepper, salt, Worcestershire sauce, and panko. Mix until just combined.

3. Split into two equal portions and place each on a sheet of plastic wrap. Shape into a cylinder about the length of the puff pastry sheet. Roll up and place in the refrigerator for at least 15 minutes.

TO ASSEMBLE:

4. Whisk together the egg and the water and set aside. Cut the puff pastry in half. Take one of the halves and roll the dough out slightly at the edges.

5. Take the prepared lamb logs out of the refrigerator and place near one end of the puff pastry. On the opposite end of the pastry, brush the egg wash. Tightly roll the sausage roll and pinch the puff pastry together.

6. Wrap in plastic wrap and place in the freezer. Repeat with the other portion. Allow to rest in the freezer for 20 minutes. Preheat the oven to 450°F.

7. Prepare a baking sheet with parchment paper and spray with nonstick spray. Take the sausage rolls out of the freezer and unwrap. Cut each into four equal pieces and place on the baking sheet. Brush each piece with egg wash.

8. Combine the white sesame seeds, black sesame seeds, and dehydrated onion flakes. Sprinkle over each of the prepared rolls.

9. Bake in the oven for 10 minutes. Reduce the heat to 350°F and bake for another 20 minutes, or until the lamb is cooked through.

87

BREW-BATTERED WEDGES

There are a few things that just go together. Hammer and steel. Coal and fire. Pentalla and me. And, of course, ale and potato. This dish is beloved in every corner of the Claim. Its simplicity may fool you into thinking it's some meek side dish, but when done right, it can steal the show. Brew-Battered Wedges should never be underestimated.

DIFFICULTY: ◆◆◇◇◇

PREP TIME: 30 minutes   **COOK TIME:** 35 minutes   **YIELD:** 6 servings   **DIETARY NOTES:** Vegan, Gluten-Free, Alcohol

One 12-ounce can light beer
5 cups water
2 sprigs thyme
1 bay leaf
1 teaspoon kosher salt
1½ pounds small golden potatoes, cut in half
2 tablespoons olive oil
1 teaspoon dried thyme
1 teaspoon garlic powder
Kosher salt, to taste
Ground black pepper, to taste

1. Preheat the oven to 425°F. Combine the beer, water, thyme sprigs, bay leaf, and salt in a medium pot. Bring to a boil and add the potatoes. Cook for 8 minutes. Drain and discard the thyme and bay leaf.

2. In a medium bowl, combine the olive oil, dried thyme, and garlic powder. Add the boiled potatoes to the bowl and toss until coated. Place the oiled potatoes on a baking sheet with parchment paper. Season with salt and pepper. Bake for 20 minutes, toss the potatoes around, and bake for another 15 minutes.

MILDUF'S TREAT

Deep-fried blazon sweetspice balls infused with honey syrup—doesn't that sound like a dish worthy of a Sun-King? This recipe requires a bit of care and skill; the dough can get sticky and harder to manage than a horde of Bristlebacks, but the bother is worth it. Occasionally, when I'm feeling particularly peeved, I like to surprise diners with a fiery overspiced ball hidden among a batch.

DIFFICULTY: ◆◆◆◇◇

PREP TIME: 30 minutes   INACTIVE TIME: 1 hour   COOK TIME: 5 minutes per batch
YIELD: 18 to 20 servings   DIETARY NOTES: Vegetarian, Dairy-Free

DOUGH
- 1 cup warm water
- 1 tablespoon vegetable oil
- 2 tablespoons honey
- 2½ teaspoons active dry yeast
- 2¼ cups all-purpose flour
- ½ teaspoon ground cardamom
- ½ teaspoon ground cinnamon
- ¼ teaspoon ground ginger
- 1 teaspoon kosher salt
- Zest of 1 lemon
- 1 teaspoon vanilla paste
- Neutral oil (such as peanut or canola), for frying

HONEY SYRUP
- ½ cup honey
- 2 tablespoons water
- ½ teaspoon kosher salt

1. Combine the water, vegetable oil, honey, and yeast in a small bowl. Let rest for 5 minutes until the yeast begins to froth. Whisk together the flour, cardamom, cinnamon, ginger, salt, and lemon zest in a large bowl.

2. Add the water mixture and vanilla paste to the large bowl. Mix until the dough just comes together. Cover with plastic wrap and let rise for 1 hour, or until doubled in size.

NOTE: *This dough will be extremely sticky. It is best to keep your hand or spatula damp when working with it. However, be careful not to get any water in the hot oil once you start frying.*

3. While the dough is rising, prepare the honey syrup by combining all ingredients in a small saucepan. Heat over medium-high heat. Once the syrup starts to boil, remove from the heat and set aside.

4. With a spatula, scrape the dough down the sides of the bowl, then cover with a damp kitchen towel. Prepare a small bowl with water and two spoons, which will be used for scooping the dough. While the dough rests, fill a deep pot with 2 inches of neutral frying oil and heat over medium heat to 350°F.

5. Once heated, take one of the spoons, shake off any excess water, and scoop a portion of dough. Use the other spoon to help form it into a rough round shape. Carefully place in the oil. Repeat with a few more portions, making sure not to overcrowd the pot.

6. Fry for 5 minutes, or until golden brown. As they cook, they will turn on their own. If not, make sure to turn them about halfway through the cooking process.

7. Remove from the oil and transfer to a plate lined with paper towels to let any excess oil drip off. Repeat these steps until all the dough has been fried.

8. Once drained, transfer all the fried balls into the honey syrup and toss to coat. These are best enjoyed the same day they're made.

SPARKALE

Might as well wrap up my Oseram recipes with the most uplifting beverage ever poured in the Claim. Sure, we Oseram love a creamy Forgefroth, but sometimes, in the scorching heat, it's nice to lighten things up with a bit of fizz and a little zest. This mixed drink leaves a refreshing finish on the tongue and always has me wanting to order another.

DIFFICULTY: ◆◇◇◇◇

PREP TIME: 5 minutes **YIELD:** 1 drink **DIETARY NOTES:** Vegetarian, Dairy-Free, Alcohol

8 ounces mead
4 ounces Ginger Lemonade (page 181)
6 ounces club soda
2 slices lemon

1. Combine the mead, ginger lemonade, and club soda in a large glass. Add the lemon slices and serve.

CARJA

— MERIDIAN —

No surprise that the Carja have gotten good at hauling loot from the Daunt back to Meridian. There's always a shipment of wood, ore, or Greenshine to hitch a ride with.

News of our journey must've been sent from Barren Light. A Vanguard awaited us in the Royal Maizelands like we were a couple of nobles. While the guard urged us on, Pentalla lingered, eyeing the fields. "These water trenches, they service the crops. The same could be done in the Lowlands." She looked over, "Scribble that down in your little scroll."

Entering Meridian through the marvelous (OSERAM!) elevator and witnessing the Palace of the Sun, one is quickly reminded there's nowhere like Meridian. And almost as quickly, one is reminded there's no tribe quite as squeamish around outlanders as the Carja.

Walking through the narrow streets, merchants whispered that we must be headed straight for a dungeon. Some scuttled at the sight of us. "Good to see the Tenakth still strike fear in the heart of the Carja," Pentalla mused.

A noble named Marad welcomed us to the Palace. He directed us to our prepared chambers, where we could leave our weapons. Pentalla took this as merely a suggestion. Finally, we were shown to the royal kitchens. I remembered I'd pined for a place in the Sun-King's cookery. All knew of its pantry—stocked with every ingredient from across the Sundom and beyond.

We were informed that Sun-King Avad had asked if we would do him the honor of preparing a meal "in the Tenakth tradition." Without hesitation, I accepted on our behalf. I would commemorate this moment with a plaque in Milduf's!

After Marad left the room, Pentalla elbowed me. "I am here to learn. Not to serve." I tried to persuade her, arguing that she's an Envoy and cooking counts as envoying.

"Fine," she conceded, disappearing into the larder. I thought she'd seen sense, but NOPE! She emerged with a bushel of redthorn pepper in one hand and two pantry rodents held by their tails in the other.

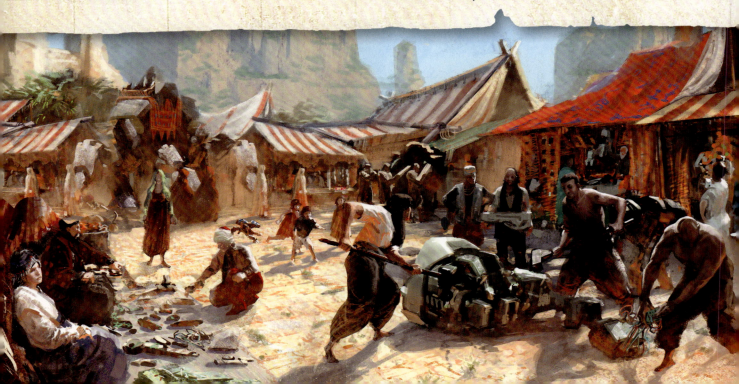

I told her there was no way we could serve rats to the Sun-King!

"It's called 'tiny meat.' Only the freshest for your glorious Sun-King." She pulled a hunting knife from her waist and slapped her catch on the chopping board. "He wants to eat as a Tenakth? In the Desert Clan, we make do."

I couldn't believe it. All the ingredients in the world. A golden opportunity to build renown. And here was Pentalla deboning rodents. And so, desperate to save the meal, I poured a dollop of kindleweed oil on her coals when she wasn't looking. Within a minute, the rats were ashen.

She saw through my ruse. Stubbornly, she insisted that they would be all she would serve and she hoped the Sun-King was blessed with strong teeth. I reminded her that I had her recipes. I could make them myself if she wouldn't.

"I regret sharing those with a cook who reduces quicker than a thin sauce." She stormed out of the kitchen, and I set to work without giving it a second thought. I prepared a mix of all I had learned, finishing each course just as the servers arrived.

Later in the kitchen, while I was picking the brains of a Carja cook, Sun-King Avad appeared. I couldn't believe it. I was laden with flour and covered in oil. He'd hoped to thank the Tenakth Envoy personally. I covered for her. I said my companion was unwell. The mesa air had gotten to her head.

As a show of appreciation, Avad offered his Vanguard to see us up to Nora territory and his personal healer, too, if that would help my Tenakth friend.

The Sun-King enjoyed my meal. But that victory felt empty. Before leaving, I made up a plate of Pentalla's favorites. Yet, once I got to her chamber, I couldn't summon the courage to knock.

What could I say? I left the food by her door. I hope it's not getting too cold.

SUN WINGS

Manning the kitchen at Chainscrape, I'd meet the occasional Carja—traders, soldiers, and even a few high-class nobles looking to hunt at the rarely seen, thrilling edge of the Sundom. Without fail, they would all ask for Sun Wings, and now, I finally know how to prepare these fiery morsels. Even the most studious of Sun-Priests can't resist getting their hands dirty with this one.

DIFFICULTY: ◆◆◇◇◇

PREP TIME: 15 minutes **INACTIVE TIME:** 30 minutes **COOK TIME:** 25 minutes
YIELD: 4 servings **DIETARY NOTES:** Dairy-Free, Gluten-Free

⅓ cup dark brown sugar
1 tablespoon Kashmiri chile powder
2 teaspoons kosher salt
2 teaspoons garlic powder
1 teaspoon onion powder
1 teaspoon sweet paprika
1 teaspoon ground coriander
1 teaspoon ground cumin
1 teaspoon ground black pepper
4 pounds chicken wings

EQUIPMENT
Grill

1. Combine the brown sugar, Kashmiri chile powder, salt, garlic powder, onion powder, paprika, coriander, cumin, and black pepper in a small bowl. Place the chicken wings in a large bowl and add the spice mixture. Toss until the wings are fully coated.

2. Transfer to a baking sheet with a wire rack. Place in the refrigerator for 30 minutes, or until the grill is preheated.

3. Preheat the grill. Make sure to have your heat source only on one side of the grill. The side with no coals (or gas) is called the indirect-heat section.

4. Place the chicken wings over the indirect-heat section of the grill. Cover the grill, leaving the cover slightly ajar. Cook for 10 minutes.

5. Remove the cover and flip the wings. Grill until the chicken is cooked through (internal temperature of 165°F), about 5 to 10 minutes.

6. Transfer to the direct-heat side and cook until slightly charred, about 1 to 2 minutes per side. Transfer to a plate and wrap in aluminum foil until served.

MESA BREAD

When I first learned of this caramel-topped bun from the Sun-King's kitchen staff, I thought surely this must be some kind of royal delicacy. Turns out, it's eaten by laborers and traders. These Carja sure know how to spoil themselves. What a decadent combination—blazon sweetspice, brown sugar, honey, syrup, plenty of butter, topped with crunchy nuts. Even writing this, I fear my drool may cause the ink to run!

DIFFICULTY: ◆◆◆◇◇

PREP: 1 hour **INACTIVE TIME:** 2 hours **COOK TIME:** 45 minutes **YIELD:** 12 buns **DIETARY NOTES:** Vegetarian

DOUGH

- 1¼ cups warmed milk (no hotter than 110°F)
- 2½ teaspoons active dry yeast
- 7 tablespoons unsalted butter, room temperature
- ¼ cup sugar
- 1 egg
- 1 egg yolk
- 1 teaspoon vanilla paste
- 4¼ cups all-purpose flour
- 1 teaspoon kosher salt

1. Combine the milk and yeast in a small bowl. In a stand mixer with a dough hook attachment, combine the butter and sugar. Once well combined, add the eggs and vanilla paste to the butter-and-sugar mixture. Then add the milk-and-yeast mixture.

2. Add the flour and salt. Mix until just combined. Take the dough out of the bowl and knead by hand for 5 minutes. Place the dough in a greased bowl and cover. Allow the dough to rise for at least 2 hours, or until it doubles in size.

3. When the dough is nearly done rising, prepare the topping. Combine the brown sugar, butter, honey, maple syrup, vanilla paste, and salt in a saucepan over medium-high heat. Heat until the sugar dissolves and everything is combined, about 5 minutes.

4. Transfer the topping to a 13-by-9-inch deep baking dish. Spread out into an even layer at the bottom. Top with the crushed nuts.

5. Prepare the dough filling by combining the brown sugar, cinnamon, nutmeg, and salt and set aside. Transfer the dough to a lightly floured work surface and roll it out into an 18-by-15-inch rectangle.

TOPPING

¾ cup dark brown sugar
½ cup unsalted butter
⅓ cup honey
2 tablespoons maple syrup
1 teaspoon vanilla paste
½ teaspoon kosher salt
½ cup pecans, toasted and crushed
½ cup walnuts, toasted and crushed

FILLING

½ cup dark brown sugar
1 tablespoon ground cinnamon
¼ teaspoon grated nutmeg
1 teaspoon kosher salt
¼ cup unsalted butter, melted

EQUIPMENT

13-by-9-inch deep baking dish

6. Brush the dough with butter, keeping a ½-inch border empty. Sprinkle the cinnamon mixture over the buttered area. Tightly roll the dough lengthwise, then use a serrated knife to cut it into 12 equal pieces. Place the pieces, cut side down, into the prepared baking dish. Cover the dish with a towel and allow the buns to rise for another 30 minutes.

7. Preheat the oven to 375°F. Remove the towel, place the baking dish in the oven, and bake for 20 minutes. Then cover with aluminum foil and bake for another 10 minutes, or until cooked through. Remove from the oven and allow to cool for 5 minutes.

8. Run a knife around the edges to loosen the buns. Carefully and quickly flip the pan onto a large serving tray. The buns should slide out of the pan, with the caramelly nut topping now on top.

GRAZER'S BOUNTY

Royal cooks tell me that some of the Sun-King's favorite recipes originated in lowly soldier's cookhouses. Rumor has it, he first tasted this spicy leaf-lover-friendly soup while exiled and planning his coup against the Mad Sun-King Jiran. After taking the throne, he brought an army field cook into his royal kitchen, ensuring he'd always have access to this flavorsome meal.

DIFFICULTY: ◆◆◇◇◇

PREP TIME: 45 minutes   **COOK TIME:** 30 minutes   **YIELD:** 6 to 8 servings   **DIETARY NOTES:** Vegan, Gluten-Free

GREEN CHILE PASTE
1 bunch cilantro
6 garlic cloves
4 scallions
1 serrano pepper
One 1-inch piece ginger
1 stalk lemongrass
1 teaspoon ground black pepper
1 teaspoon ground cumin
½ teaspoon ground coriander
1½ teaspoons kosher salt
1 teaspoon sugar
Zest and juice of 3 limes
2 teaspoons canola oil

SOUP
1 tablespoon canola oil
1 red onion, sliced
½ pound baby potato medley
3 carrots, peeled and cut into bite-size pieces
2 cups vegetable broth
1 head broccoli, cut into bite-size pieces
½ head cauliflower, cut into bite-size pieces
Green chile paste
30 ounces coconut milk
Cilantro, chopped, for garnish
Cooked rice or udon, for serving (optional)
Lime slices, for garnish

TO MAKE THE GREEN CHILE PASTE:
1. In a food processor, add all the ingredients for the chile paste and pulse until it reaches the consistency of a thick paste. Store in the refrigerator until you are ready to use it for the soup. It should be good for up to 1 week.

TO MAKE THE SOUP:
2. Heat a large pot with the canola oil over medium-high heat. Add the onion and cook until softened, about 5 minutes. Add the potatoes and carrots, toss together, and cook for 5 minutes to slightly heat the vegetables.

3. Add the vegetable broth. Bring to a boil, then reduce the heat to a simmer. Place the lid slightly ajar and simmer for 10 minutes. Add the broccoli and cauliflower and simmer for 10 more minutes, or until the cauliflower has softened.

4. Add the chile paste and coconut milk and mix well. Cook for 3 more minutes.

5. Serve in a bowl with cooked rice or udon. Top with cilantro and lime slices.

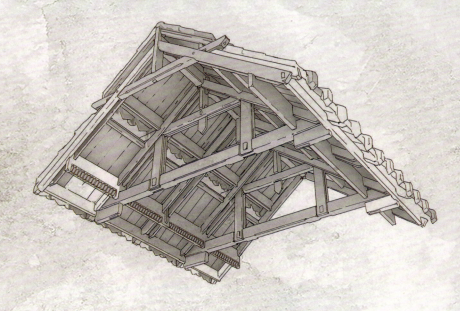

SUN-SEARED RIBS

Tender, lean ribs slathered in a smoky grill sauce. This is a dish that anyone but an Utaru dreams about, right? Though every tribe's got their way of preparing this cut of meat, what makes the Carja's stand out is the sour, tangy marinade, with a sharp spice rub added for good measure.

DIFFICULTY: ◆◆◇◇◇

PREP TIME: 20 minutes **INACTIVE TIME:** 4 hours **COOK TIME:** 3½ to 4½ hours
YIELD: 1 rack of ribs **DIETARY NOTES:** Dairy-Free, Gluten-Free

3 tablespoons dark brown sugar
2 tablespoons kosher salt
1 tablespoon paprika
1 tablespoon garlic powder
1 tablespoon onion powder
1 teaspoon ground mustard
1 teaspoon dried oregano
1 teaspoon cayenne pepper
1 tablespoon mustard
1 tablespoon rice vinegar
½ teaspoon liquid smoke
1 rack baby back ribs, membrane removed
½ to 1 cup barbecue sauce

1. Combine the brown sugar, salt, paprika, garlic powder, onion powder, ground mustard, oregano, and cayenne pepper in a medium bowl.

2. Combine the mustard, rice vinegar, and liquid smoke in a small bowl. Brush all parts of the ribs with the wet mixture, then rub the spice mixture onto the ribs, likewise making sure not to miss any parts. Place onto a large sheet of aluminum foil, wrap the foil around the ribs, and seal completely closed. Place in the refrigerator and allow to marinate for 4 hours.

3. Prepare a baking sheet with a wire rack. Preheat the oven to 300°F. While the oven is preheating, take the ribs out of the refrigerator and let rest at room temperature for 15 minutes.

4. Place the aluminum-foil-wrapped ribs (keep them completely sealed) on the wire rack. Transfer the baking sheet to the oven and bake for 3 to 4 hours, or until the ribs are tender.

5. Remove from the oven and increase the heat to 450°F. Open the aluminum foil to brush the ribs generously with barbecue sauce. Leave the aluminum foil open and place back in the oven to bake for another 10 minutes.

6. Remove from the oven and carefully rewrap the ribs with the aluminum foil. Allow the meat to rest for 10 minutes before slicing.

NOTE: *Your butcher can remove the membrane from the ribs for you.*

ROYAL GRITS

Named for the Royal Maizefields, where its main ingredient grows readily, these grits are a staple side for many Carja meals, including Sun-Seared Ribs. But as with everything Carja, there must be added flair, and so, even this simple side incorporates delicious fowl broth, potent spices, and onion ground to a powder. In a way, I have to tip my cap to them.

DIFFICULTY: ◆◆◇◇◇

PREP TIME: 10 minutes COOK TIME: 20 minutes YIELD: 2 to 3 servings DIETARY NOTES: N/A

2 cups chicken broth
½ cup milk
2 tablespoons unsalted butter
1 teaspoon onion powder
½ teaspoon ground turmeric
½ cup stone-ground yellow corn grits
¼ cup yellow cheddar cheese, shredded
Kosher salt, to taste
Ground black pepper, to taste

1. Combine the broth, milk, butter, onion powder, and turmeric in a medium pot. Bring to a boil over medium-high heat.

NOTE: *Keep an eye on the pot, because the milk can easily cause the mixture to boil over.*

2. Slowly add the grits while whisking continually. Once all the grits are added, whisk for another 2 minutes. Reduce the heat to low and cover. Simmer for 15 to 20 minutes, or until cooked. Make sure to stir from time to time to prevent the grits from sticking to the bottom of the pot.

3. Add the cheese and mix until just combined. Season with salt and pepper. Split into portions and serve with additional butter on top.

BLAZED BEANS

Yet another fantastic way to make your greens more palatable or even, dare I say, delicious. Just toss beans with oil and spices in a bowl. Really slosh it around. Then, tumble it onto a steel sheet for baking. Twenty minutes under a roaring fire, and you've got a tray of tasty bites. If only some people were as simple to deal with as these beans!

DIFFICULTY: ◆♢♢♢♢

PREP TIME: 20 minutes **COOK TIME:** 20 minutes **YIELD:** 6 to 8 servings **DIETARY NOTES:** Vegan, Gluten-Free

2 pounds green beans
2 tablespoons olive oil
2 teaspoons light brown sugar
1 teaspoon kosher salt
1 teaspoon ground black pepper
4 garlic cloves, chopped

1. Preheat the oven to 425°F. Prepare a large baking sheet with parchment paper. Combine the green beans, olive oil, brown sugar, salt, and pepper in a large bowl. Toss until the green beans are completely coated. Transfer to the prepared baking sheet.

2. Bake in the oven for 15 minutes. Add the garlic and toss to coat. Return to the oven and bake for another 3 to 5 minutes, or until the green beans are tender.

SUNFALL MAIZEMEAT

I bet this dish got its name from how long it takes—by the time you're done with the three-hour prep and the two-hour cook, the sun's probably fallen! Personally, I find the entire process soothing. Pentalla, on the other hand, considered it "'unnecessarily indulgent." But isn't that nice sometimes?!

DIFFICULTY: ◆◆◆◆◆

PREP TIME: 3 hours **INACTIVE TIME:** 12 Hours **COOK TIME:** 2 hours
YIELD: 18 to 20 tamales **DIETARY NOTES:** Dairy-Free, Gluten-Free

POACHED CHICKEN

2 chicken breasts
¼ onion, sliced
2 bay leaves
1 chicken bouillon cube
1 tablespoon black peppercorns

TOMATILLO SALSA

13 tomatillos, husks removed and cut in half
5 garlic cloves
1 serrano pepper, cut in half and seeds removed
1 poblano pepper, cut in half and seeds removed
½ onion
1 bunch cilantro
2 scallions
3 limes, juiced
1 teaspoon kosher salt
1 teaspoon ground black pepper

TO MAKE THE POACHED CHICKEN:

1. Place the chicken breasts, onion, bay leaves, chicken bouillon, and black peppercorns in a small pot. Fill with water until the chicken is covered. Place over medium-high heat and bring to a boil. Lower heat to low and simmer for 10 to 15 minutes, until the chicken registers an internal temperature of 165°F. Remove the chicken from the water and wrap in aluminum foil until needed. Once the chicken has cooled, shred it by hand.

2. Drain the water and reserve the liquid for a broth later in the recipe.

TO MAKE THE TOMATILLO SALSA:

3. Preheat the oven broiler. Place the tomatillos, garlic, both peppers, and onion on a baking sheet. Put the baking sheet under the broiler and cook until the tomatillos have charred slightly, about 10 minutes.

4. Remove from the oven and allow to cool. Transfer to a food processor. Add the cilantro, scallions, lime juice, salt, and pepper. Pulse the food processor until smooth. Season with additional salt and pepper if needed. Can be stored in an airtight container in the refrigerator for up to 1 week.

5. To finish the filling, combine the shredded chicken breast with 1 cup of salsa. Set aside until you are ready to fill the tamales.

MASA

30 corn husks

3½ cups instant masa harina

2 teaspoons baking powder

2 teaspoons kosher salt

1/4 cup Tomatillo Salsa

2½ cups chicken broth, from the poached chicken

8 ounces vegetable shortening

EQUIPMENT

Deep steamer basket

TO MAKE THE MASA:

6. Place the corn husks in a large bowl and fill with enough water to cover. Let rest overnight to rehydrate.

7. Combine the masa harina, baking powder, and salt in a medium bowl. Add the salsa and chicken broth and mix until crumbly. Cover with a wet towel and set aside.

8. Place the vegetable shortening in the bowl of a stand mixer with a paddle attachment. Whip the shortening on medium speed for about 5 minutes to make it light and fluffy. Scrape the sides of the bowl from time to time to make sure all the shortening is being whipped.

9. Add the masa mixture. Set the stand mixer to medium speed and whip until fluffy, about 10 minutes. Again, make sure to scrape the sides down as it is being worked. If the mixture is a bit too dry, add water.

NOTE: *One way to test if your dough is ready is to fill a glass with water. Take a teaspoon of the dough and place it in the water. If it floats, the dough is airy enough for the tamales.*

10. Once mixed, remove from the stand mixer and cover with a wet towel.

11. To assemble a tamale, take one of the corn husks and pat dry. Have the smooth side facing up and the wide part at the top. Spread 2 ounces of the masa over the top half with a moistened spoon, forming a thin rectangle. Place about 1 tablespoon of the chicken filling in the center of the masa.

12. Fold the husk vertically, wrapping the masa around the filling. Take the other side and fold it shut like a trifold brochure, creating a long tube shape. Fold the bottom half of the husk up. You can use a small strip of corn husk to tie the bottom shut. Place on a baking sheet and cover with a wet towel.

13. Repeat Steps 11 and 12 until all the tamales are prepared.

14. Prepare a large pot with a deep steamer basket. Fill with 2 inches of water, making sure the steamer basket doesn't touch the water. Carefully place the tamales in the steamer basket, open side facing upward.

NOTE: *It is important that the tamales are standing up during the steaming process. If needed, add a heatproof bowl or ball of aluminum foil to keep them upright.*

15. Cover the tamales with the extra pieces of husk and a wet towel. Finally, cover the pot with a lid, place over medium-high heat, and bring the water to a boil. Once boiling, reduce the heat and allow to simmer for 60 to 90 minutes, or until the tamales are cooked through. To test if the tamales are done, try opening one—if the husk pulls away easily from the tamale, it is cooked through.

SUNGRIA

Maybe the Carja don't brew with quite the same gusto as us Oseram, but they sure know what they're doing with their grapes. This drink is infused with every fruit under their precious Sun, turning the heaviest of evening reds into a delightfully light tipple that one could enjoy at the peak of a summer's day while gazing at mesa views. Sharing a pitcher would've been a nice way to cap things off with Pentalla…

DIFFICULTY: ◆◇◇◇◇

PREP TIME: 20 minutes   **INACTIVE TIME:** 1 hour   **YIELD:** 4 to 6 servings
DIETARY NOTES: Vegan, Gluten-Free, Alcohol

- 1 Granny Smith apple, sliced
- 1 pear, sliced
- 1 blood orange, sliced and quartered
- ½ cup pomegranate arils
- 2 tablespoons light brown sugar
- ¼ cup orange liqueur
- 1 tablespoon elderflower liqueur
- One 750-milliliter (25-ounce) bottle dry red wine
- 1 cup pomegranate juice
- ¾ cup orange juice
- Ice, for serving

1. Combine all the ingredients in a pitcher and stir together.
2. Refrigerate for at least 1 hour. Serve over ice with extra fruit if desired.

NORA

— VALLEYMEET —

On this leg of our journey, Pentalla was pricklier than usual. While she hunted turkey in the Gatelands, I picked some Wild Ember for seasoning, but she refused to use it. When I told a hilarious Carja joke at Lone Light, she ignored it. And when, at Daytower, I procured directions from a Nora huntress, Pentalla only grunted approval.

Thanks to the well-documented exploits of a certain redhead, whom I consider a close friend, the Nora's Sacred Lands had recently opened. Although, I gathered outlanders were still somewhat of a rarity, as the young huntress seemed excited by the novelty of speaking to an Oseram. She spoke of a once-renowned cook nearby. Just as it seemed I'd struck easy ore, her voice turned grave. "Fens lives as an outcast by choice in the wooded outskirts of the Forsaken Village, where our people do not dare tread."

Now, I'm not superstitious, but at night, those trees take the shape of all manner of horrors. I stuck close behind Pentalla as we trod carefully through the woods, dodging the glow of patrolling Watchers' eyes.

Eventually, we found the warm light of a small campfire beside which an elder Nora warmed his hands. I approached carefully and asked if he was Fens, the Master Cook. The elderly Nora frowned. "All-Mother creates the land, the animals, the plants. I simply rearrange her creations." He carefully placed a stick in the fire. We'd come a long way, I explained, hoping he would teach us his recipes.

"Here's a lesson." He pointed toward the two of us. "Some ingredients shouldn't mix. Reason I'm short a village is outlanders. Your 'mission' will not send me running for my cookpot."

Pentalla frowned. I worried she'd scare Fens off by drawing a weapon. But instead, she sat beside him. "Until recently, my tribe greeted outsiders with a blade." She

looked at me. "Sometimes, we still do. For generations, we didn't even trust our comrades from other clans." She added another stick to the fire. "But times have changed, and we're stronger for what we share."

Fens looked to the sky as the clouds parted, revealing the stars. "The sparks of the Goddess' fire… a positive omen." He brushed a lock of light grey matted hair from his eyes, then stood slowly and headed into the woods. "Come. If you wish to eat, we must forage. And we must hunt."

And so, in the night, we scoured the Valleymeet, learning the old man's ways. We found a fieldbird resting in a clearing. Fens pulled a sling from his side and a stone from the earth. He fired, knocking the bird out, all without the rustle of a single leaf.

Eventually, he led us to an abandoned settlement. The decrepit buildings were made with thick logs lashed together, and beautiful but aged ornaments hung from their eaves. Behind one of these cabins, Fens unearthed a hidden trove of oils, ground spices, and pots.

I couldn't help but shudder in this haunted place. Noting my discomfort, Fens explained, "This is the only place I ever cooked. The only place I'll ever cook." So, in the center of the Forsaken Village, that's what we did. With the bird, we prepared Fieldbird Stew, a dish that requires patience. During the many hours the fowl stewed, Fens talked of his people. The Nora spend much of their lives under the open sky and eat communally. Though, from how he picked his ears with a bird bone, it was clear Fens had lacked company for some time.

The meat was hearty and gushing with flavor, falling apart as I bit into it. It had been a long night, and the food knocked us out like a Charger's kick. We rested well into the daytime.

When we awoke in the sunlight, surrounded by the green majesty of the Sacred Lands, Fens was gone.

VALLEYCAKES

Our time with Fens flew by too quickly. Though he'd talked me through this recipe, I could only attempt to recreate it from the notes I'd scribbled down. It was a breakfast food that was flat as this valley floor—sweet and fluffy, yet hardy enough to get a Nora through a long day of hunting and foraging. The drizzle of berry sauce is my own added touch.

DIFFICULTY: ◆◆◇◇◇

PREP: 30 minutes   INACTIVE TIME: 8 hours   COOK TIME: 45 minutes
YIELD: 4 servings   DIETARY NOTES: Vegetarian, Dairy-Free

LINGONBERRY COMPOTE
2 cups frozen lingonberries
⅓ cup sugar
⅓ cup water
1 teaspoon kosher salt

PANCAKES
1 large sweet potato, shredded
½ onion, shredded
¼ cup all-purpose flour
1 egg
1 teaspoon kosher salt
Neutral oil (such as peanut or canola), for frying

TO MAKE THE LINGONBERRY COMPOTE:
1. Place all the ingredients in a medium saucepan over medium-high heat and mix together well. Allow the mixture to start bubbling, then mash the fruit. Reduce the heat to medium-low and cook for 30 minutes, or until the mixture has slightly thickened. Transfer to an airtight container and allow to cool. Cover and place in the refrigerator overnight.

TO MAKE THE PANCAKES:
2. Combine the sweet potato, onion, flour, egg, and salt in a bowl.
3. Heat a medium-size pan with ⅛ inch of neutral oil over medium-high heat. Once the oil is heated, take a handful of the potato mixture and form into a small pancake, about ¼ inch thick.
4. Carefully place the pancake in the oil, making sure not to overcrowd the pan. Cook each side for 4 to 5 minutes, or until each side is golden brown. Once cooked, transfer to a plate lined with paper towels. Repeat until all of the potato mixture has been cooked.

119

FORAGER'S POUCH

According to Fens, this bread pouch can be stuffed with many delights. It is a favorite of patrolling hunters, who assemble them fresh in the wilds. The Sacred Lands are bountiful, and each Nora settlement prefers its own variation of fillings. Fens likes his meat-free, with hearty fruit, beans, clean peppery herbs, and a tangy cheese sauce.

DIFFICULTY: ◆◆◆◇◇

PREP: 45 minutes   COOK TIME: 30 minutes   YIELD: 4 arepas   DIETARY NOTES: Vegetarian

PLÁTANOS FRITOS

2 plantains, very ripe
Kosher salt
Neutral oil (such as peanut or canola), for frying

BLACK BEANS

1 tablespoon olive oil
½ onion, chopped
One 15-ounce can black beans, liquid strained
1 teaspoon ground cumin
1 teaspoon ground coriander

TO MAKE THE PLÁTANOS FRITOS:

1. Prepare the plantains by cutting them open and slicing into ½-inch-thick pieces. Lightly salt.

2. Fill a frying pan with ½ inch of oil and heat over medium heat. Once heated, carefully add the plantains and cook each side until golden, about 2 to 3 minutes per side.

3. Transfer to a paper towel on a plate to drain excess oil. Don't leave them on the paper towel for too long, or they can get stuck.

TO MAKE THE BLACK BEANS:

4. Heat a medium saucepan over medium-high heat. Add the olive oil and onion. Cook until the onion has softened, about 8 minutes.

5. Add the black beans, cumin, and coriander. Mix well, reduce the heat to medium-low, and simmer for 10 minutes. Remove from the heat, cover, and set aside until the arepas are cooked.

AREPAS
1¼ cups warm water
Pinch of salt
1 cup areparina flour
Butter, for the pan

FOR ASSEMBLY
Queso fresco, crumbled
Cilantro, chopped

TO MAKE THE AREPAS:
6. Combine the warm water and salt in a large bowl. Add the areparina and mix in with your hands. The dough should not stick to your hands and be relatively thick. Allow to rest for 3 minutes.

7. Split the dough into 4 equal portions and form each into thick disks. Prepare a pan by rubbing butter all over it. Place the arepas on the pan.

8. Turn the heat to medium, then tightly seal the pan with aluminum foil and a pan lid. Cook for 5 to 8 minutes. Uncover and check if the bottoms have turned golden brown. If not, cover and cook until golden brown. Once flipped, allow to cook uncovered until that side is also golden brown. Take off the heat and set aside to slightly cool.

TO ASSEMBLE:
9. Once the arepas are cool enough to handle, cut them open. Place a few slices of plantain on top of the bottom piece. Top with black beans, queso fresco, and cilantro. Place the other piece of the arepa on top and serve immediately.

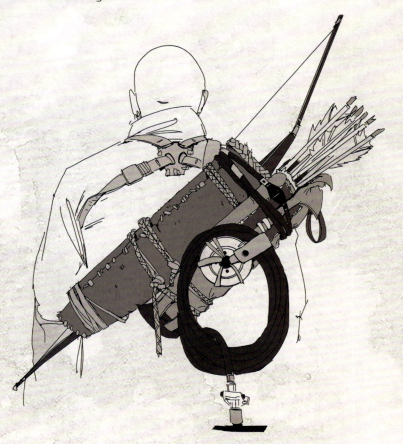

REDTHICKET BUNS

According to Fens, the two swirls of this bun represent the intertwined relationship between All-Mother, who provides generously, and the Nora, who guard her and her lands. I managed to harvest a few of the sweet-and-sour redthicket berries before we left the Sacred Lands. With some luck, the seeds within will grow into strong trees in the Claim.

DIFFICULTY: ◆◆◆◆◇

PREP TIME: 1 hour   INACTIVE TIME: 1½ hours   COOK TIME: 12 minutes   YIELD: 10 buns   DIETARY NOTES: Vegetarian

DOUGH
½ teaspoon saffron threads
⅓ cup sugar
1 cup milk
3½ cups bread flour
2¼ teaspoons active dry yeast
1½ teaspoons kosher salt
½ teaspoon ground cardamom (optional)
1 egg, room temperature
6 tablespoons unsalted butter, room temperature

1. Combine the saffron and 1 tablespoon of sugar in a mortar and pestle. Grind until the saffron becomes a powder. Transfer to a medium saucepan with the milk. Heat over medium-high heat and bring to a simmer. Remove from the heat and allow to cool until the mixture reduces in temperature to 100° to 110°F.

2. Combine the remaining sugar, flour, yeast, salt, and cardamom in a large bowl. Add the cooled saffron-milk mixture and egg to the bowl and mix until the dough just comes together.

3. While beginning to knead the dough, add the butter 1 tablespoon at a time. Knead for 10 minutes. If the dough is too sticky, add 1 tablespoon of flour at a time. If it is too dry, add 1 tablespoon of milk at a time.

4. Transfer to an oiled bowl, cover, and let rest for 1 hour, or until the dough has doubled in size. Once doubled, punch down and knead. Line a baking sheet with parchment paper.

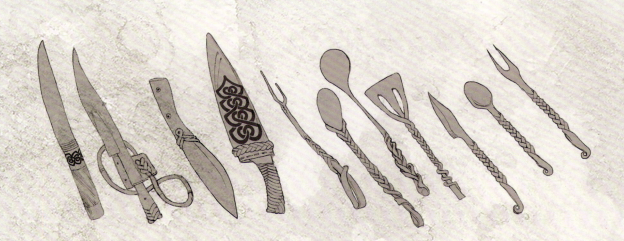

125

FOR ASSEMBLY
1 egg
2 tablespoons milk
20 dried cherries

EQUIPMENT
Mortar and pestle

5. Divide the dough into 10 equal portions. Shape into round balls and place under a kitchen towel.

6. Take one of the dough balls and roll out flat until it is about 1 inch thick. Take one end and tightly roll the dough into a log. Using your hands, roll the log until it is about 10 to 12 inches long. If the dough is resisting and not rolling out, place it back under the kitchen towel and allow to rest for 10 minutes.

7. Once rolled out, twist the two opposite ends in opposite directions to shape into two spirals connected together at the center, like an S. Place on the prepared baking sheet and cover with a kitchen towel.

8. Repeat Steps 6 and 7 with the remaining portions.

9. Once all the buns have been prepared, keep the tray covered and allow to rise for about 30 minutes, or until doubled in size.

10. Preheat the oven to 400°F. Whisk together the egg and milk. Carefully brush each of the buns. Place a dried cherry in the center of each of the spirals.

11. Bake in the oven for 10 to 12 minutes, or until slightly golden brown and cooked through.

GODDESS' GOLD

Though the Nora love their meat—their hunting skills are renowned even beyond the borders of these Sacred Lands—their diet is balanced with a whole lot of leaf-lover-friendly options. This spicy dish combines a solid base of starchy chopped vegetables and greens. It's served as an accompaniment to Fens' Fieldbird Stew.

DIFFICULTY: ◆◆◇◇◇

PREP TIME: 15 minutes **COOK TIME:** 30 minutes **YIELD:** 6 to 8 servings
DIETARY NOTES: Vegan, Gluten-Free

1 tablespoon canola oil
1 onion, chopped
One 1-inch piece ginger, grated
2 garlic cloves, minced
1 serrano pepper, minced
1 carrot, thinly sliced
1 teaspoon ground coriander
1 teaspoon ground cumin
½ teaspoon ground turmeric
½ teaspoon ground fenugreek
¼ teaspoon ground cinnamon
1 teaspoon kosher salt
½ green cabbage, thinly sliced
2 golden potatoes, chopped
½ cup water

1. Heat a medium pot with the canola oil over medium-high heat. Add the onion and cook until softened, about 5 to 8 minutes. Add the ginger, garlic, and serrano pepper and cook for another 3 minutes.

2. Add the carrot, coriander, cumin, turmeric, fenugreek, cinnamon, and salt. Mix in until well combined and cook for 5 minutes. Mix in the cabbage and potatoes. Add the water and cover the pot. Allow to cook for 15 minutes, or until the potatoes have softened.

NOTE: *As this cooks, the cabbage will reduce in size. Make sure to stir often so everything cooks evenly.*

3. Once the potatoes are soft, check that everything is well combined, and season with additional salt.

CRUNCHLEAF BOWL

The texture of a handful of mushy leaves might get Utaru stomachs rumbling, but certainly not an Oseram's. This is why most salads go down like a drunken delver at most gatherings in the Claim. None of those problems here. Two types of nuts, three sorts of berries, and crumbled mountain goat cheese bring a satisfying texture to this quick salad.

DIFFICULTY: ◆◆◇◇◇

PREP: 30 minutes   YIELD: 4 servings   DIETARY NOTES: Vegetarian

DRESSING
¼ cup rice vinegar
¼ cup honey
¼ cup lemon juice
2 teaspoons Dijon mustard
1 teaspoon onion powder
⅓ cup olive oil
1 tablespoon poppy seeds

SALAD
10 ounces baby spring mix
4 ounces raspberries
4 ounces blueberries
4 ounces blackberries
⅓ cup walnuts, chopped
⅓ cup pecans, chopped
4 ounces goat cheese, crumbled

TO MAKE THE DRESSING:
1. Place all the ingredients in an airtight container. Shake until mixed together. Can be stored in the refrigerator for up to 1 week.

TO MAKE THE SALAD:
2. Split the baby spring mix between four medium serving bowls. Top with raspberries, blueberries, blackberries, walnuts, pecans, and goat cheese. Dress with the dressing.

FENS' FIELDBIRD STEW

This wonderful stew is hot as a lit forge, though I imagine the prep and cooking might test my patience. Any fleshy bird will do, but the fieldbird is preferable for its plump thighs. This recipe certainly won't be made to order—with an hour of prep and two more hours to cook, my diners would hurl their ale mugs in discontent—but I could see prepped, simmering batches selling out fast.

DIFFICULTY: ◆◆◇◇◇

PREP: 1 hour **COOK TIME:** 2½ hours **YIELD:** 6 servings **DIETARY NOTES:** Dairy-Free, Gluten-Free

3 pounds chicken drumsticks and thighs, skinless
Juice of 2 lemons
1 tablespoon white vinegar
¼ cup vegetable oil
1 red onion, sliced
2 onions, sliced
2 teaspoons kosher salt
6 garlic cloves, puréed
One 3-inch piece ginger, puréed
¼ cup berbere
2 tablespoons paprika
1 tablespoon tomato paste
¼ cup clarified butter
6 hard-boiled eggs, deshelled

1. Place the chicken in a large bowl. Cover with enough water to completely submerge the chicken. Add the lemon juice and white vinegar. Mix to combine. Let rest at room temperature until needed.

NOTE: *This should only sit out for about 1 hour. Do not start unless you are ready.*

2. Heat a large pot with 1 tablespoon vegetable oil over medium heat. Add the onions and toss until coated with the oil. Cook the onions until they turn translucent, about 2 minutes.

3. Add a pinch of salt, stir, and reduce the heat to medium-low. Continue cooking and stirring occasionally until the onions become golden and caramelized, about 40 to 60 minutes.

4. Add the garlic and ginger and toss to coat. Add the remaining vegetable oil, berbere, paprika, tomato paste, salt, and ¼ cup water. Mix until well combined.

5. Drain the chicken from the water and rinse off. Cut a few slashes into the chicken, then place in the pot. Once all of the chicken is added, toss until coated in the sauce. Add 1½ cups of water.

6. Cover the pot and simmer for 40 to 60 minutes, or until the chicken is cooked.

7. Once cooked through, add the clarified butter and mix in well. Add the hard-boiled eggs and cook for another 5 to 10 minutes.

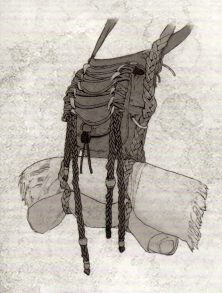

MATRIARCH'S JOY

Fens spoke incessantly of this dessert as we cooked his stew. His favorite treat for its simplicity, it brings together berries, currants, and sweetbean over medium to high heat. In a small bowl covered by a large leaf, placed beside the smoldering fire, we found he'd left us a portion to taste before disappearing into the woods.

DIFFICULTY: ◆◇◇◇◇

PREP: 15 minutes   **COOK TIME:** 15 minutes   **YIELD:** 4 servings   **DIETARY NOTES:** Vegan

6 ounces raspberries
4 ounces blackberries
4 ounces strawberries, hulled and sliced
4 ounces red currants
½ cup sugar
Pinch of salt
1 vanilla bean, split open and seeds scraped
1 cup water
2 tablespoons cornstarch
Coconut cream, for topping

1. Place the raspberries, blackberries, strawberries, currants, sugar, salt, vanilla bean and seeds, and ¾ cup of water in a medium pot. Heat over medium-high heat and bring to a boil. Reduce the heat and simmer for 15 minutes. Remove the vanilla pod and smash the berries slightly.

2. Whisk the remaining water and cornstarch together in a small bowl. Add to the pot of berries and whisk in until the mixture has thickened.

3. Serve in four bowls and top with coconut cream.

BANUK

— SONG'S EDGE —

The green woodlands gave way to icy cliffs, on which murals pointed us upwards to the Cut. The climbing, Journal. The climbing! It's like these Banuk didn't want to be found. With numb fingers, through snow and fog, we reached a ledge just moments before a far-off horn heralded a heavy blizzard.

Odd lanterns made of glowing blue machine wire dotted a path to a cave. Inside, we waited for the storm to pass. Contrary to the frigid clime, at least Pentalla was warming back up to me. "I don't like caves, Milduf. I detest frost. We've been eating trail mix for days. The moment this storm breaks, we hunt. A nice ... fatty ... mountain goat." She shivered. "We'll make a meal of it. Us two."

We emerged to knee-deep snow, and I couldn't keep up with Pentalla as she charged for her prey. Moments after she slipped out of sight, I heard her battle cry, a thing of wonder and far too terrifying for a simple goat hunt.

I ran to find Pentalla flung across a clearing, spear drawn. A gigantic Frostclaw tore through the snow, closing in on her. I rummaged through my pouch for a weapon. Bitter Leaf bushel, no. Baby potato, not this time. Then, I saw it—my trusty griddle!

Without a second thought, I slammed it against a cliff face. The heavy metal sounded loudly against the rock, and a layer of ice let off a satisfying crack. The Frostclaw turned. As I continued to bang the griddle, it charged at me, and I realized that maybe I should've had more of a plan.

The machine lunged. I tumbled out of its path, and it barreled into the cliff face. Once more, the ice cracked. This time, a shelf of snow and stone tumbled down, burying the machine under a pile of rock.

I scrambled over to Pentalla. "Milduf! You did… something!" Her expression was a big helping of shock mixed with a dash of impressed. I wish I could have savored that moment. Unfortunately, the rockpile began to shift as the Frostclaw, now without plating, threw the rocks off itself.

It began to charge once more. Pentalla fired arrows. One to its knee. Another to its belly. It slowed but didn't stop. We were cornered. I thought for sure I was seeing the forge fires of my life burning before my eyes. Turns

out, it was a volley of Fire Bursters miraculously raining down from overhead! The machine was hit and turned to flee but only made it halfway across the field before collapsing into flames.

A group of Banuk descended from the cliffs above. A shaman with glowing wire woven into her skin knelt over the machine and whispered some words before approaching us. While her hunter companions harvested the machine, we explained our mission to her. "It seems the Blue Light has guided you to us. We can lead you from here."

We were taken to a place called Song's Edge. The settlement is a constantly shifting sea of tents. The wind whistled through the calm of the camp as inkers took their time dying pelts vivid colors, and a single cook sat calmly beside a flickering fire.

The Banuk are nomads, and so their food needs to travel as well as they do. It's often cold and tough. One delicious exception is a cozy dessert known as Blue Light Pudding—the cook, impressed by our tale, prepared this for us.

And wouldn't you know it, there was an Oseram outpost there, too! Friendly enough traders. They gave us a discounted price to sleep on their cabin floor and offered a ride to Mainspring on the next convoy. I thought that sounded great, but Pentalla stayed silent.

On the morning of our departure, I noticed Pentalla's belongings weren't in the caravan. I asked why she wasn't packed and ready to go.

"I already know the food of the Oseram, Milduf. You've taught me well. I must return to the Clan Lands with the intel I've gathered." She looked away. "And, it means your punishment as my guide is complete."

I said it hadn't felt too much like a punishment to me, and she paused. I don't know if she was waiting for me to say something else. But I couldn't form the words I needed, like molten steel without a mold. I mustered a jumbled monologue about the big forge in Mainspring, and maybe she wanted to see that.

"Mmm," she continued, "I miss the desert. I might hug the first spikestalk I see." And so, we set off in our separate directions, never to see one another again.

You should strike metal when it's hot. And, Journal, I missed that swing of the hammer.

CURED COLDWATER FISH

This staple fish is as delicious as it is functional. Using this unique method of "burying" saltwater fish in various flavorful and potent spices, the Banuk are able to preserve their catch. It stays good for two, maybe even three moons, if they are able to keep it in its frozen state. Sadly, nothing sticks around forever, no matter how much we may want it to… Anyway… It's best served on Shatterbread.

DIFFICULTY: ◆◆◇◇◇

PREP: 30 minutes INACTIVE TIME: 48 hours YIELD: 4 servings DIETARY NOTES: Gluten-Free

GRAVLAX

1 pound salmon (center-cut portion, not a section near the tail)
1 tablespoon whole black peppercorns
2 teaspoons whole pink peppercorns
1 teaspoon caraway seeds
3.2 ounces kosher salt (measured by weight to equal 20% of the salmon's weight)
1 tablespoon lemon zest
1 teaspoon orange zest
1 ounce fresh dill, chopped

TO MAKE THE GRAVLAX:

1. Remove any pin bones and fatty parts from the piece of salmon and set aside.

2. Place the peppercorns and caraway seeds in a mortar and pestle and grind to slightly crush. Transfer to a medium bowl and combine with the salt, sugar, lemon zest, and orange zest.

3. Lay a large sheet of plastic wrap on a work surface. Place half of the salt mixture in the center and shape it into the size of the salmon. Top with half of the dill.

4. Place the salmon directly on top. Cover with the remaining salt mixture, making sure all parts of the salmon are coated. Finally, top with the remaining dill.

5. Carefully and tightly wrap the salmon in the plastic wrap to seal. Place it skin side up in a deep dish to prevent any liquid from making a mess. Place in the refrigerator and let rest for 24 hours.

6. The next day, flip the package over and let rest for another 24 hours.

7. Once the curing is finished, unwrap from the plastic wrap and scrape off the extra salt mixture. Rinse under cold water to remove any large bits. The cured salmon can be stored, whole, in an airtight container for up to 3 days.

CREAM CHEESE SPREAD

8 ounces cream cheese, room temperature
2 tablespoons unsalted butter, room temperature
1½ tablespoons horseradish
Zest and juice of 1 lemon
Pinch of ground black pepper
Pinch of kosher salt

PICKLED RED ONION

½ cup white vinegar
½ cup water
⅓ cup sugar
1 teaspoon kosher salt
2 bay leaves
2 teaspoons caraway seeds
1 teaspoon whole black peppercorns
1 teaspoon whole pink peppercorns
1 red onion, sliced

FOR ASSEMBLY (PER SERVING)

1 slice Shatterbread (page 143)
1 hard-boiled egg, sliced

EQUIPMENT

Mortar and pestle

TO MAKE THE CREAM CHEESE SPREAD:

8. Whisk the cream cheese and butter together in a medium bowl.

9. Add the other ingredients and mix until just combined. Season with additional salt and pepper if needed. Place in an airtight container. Can be stored in the refrigerator for up to 1 week.

TO MAKE THE PICKLED RED ONION:

10. Combine the vinegar, water, sugar, and salt in a large airtight container. Add the remaining ingredients. Cover and place in the refrigerator for at least 30 minutes. Can be stored in the refrigerator for about 1 week.

TO ASSEMBLE:

11. Using a serrated knife, cut several slices, at an angle, of gravlax. Do not cut through the skin, leaving that off the slices.

12. Spread a generous portion of the cream cheese spread on the Shatterbread. Top with sliced hard-boiled egg, gravlax, and pickled red onion. Serve as an open-faced sandwich.

SHATTERBREAD

This dish's name comes from its texture: it's crisp and easy to snap into chunks. The first morning I awoke on the cold floor of the Oseram traders' hut in Song's Edge, my discomfort was partially soothed by the malty, sweet aroma of this crumbly cracker baking. Though hearty and long-lasting, the sweet berries and honey make this crispbread not only functional but enjoyable.

DIFFICULTY: ◆◆◇◇◇

PREP: 30 minutes   INACTIVE TIME: 1 hour   COOK TIME: 1 hour   YIELD: 30 servings   DIETARY NOTES: Vegetarian

2 tablespoons honey
2¼ cups warm water
1 cup dark rye flour
1¼ cups old-fashioned oats
⅓ cup wheat bran
⅓ cup wheat berries
¼ cup rye berries
½ cup white sesame seeds
¼ cup black sesame seeds
⅓ cup pumpkin seeds, chopped
¼ cup flaxseed
1 tablespoon kosher salt

1. Whisk together the honey and water in a medium bowl. Combine the rye flour, oats, wheat bran, wheat berries, rye berries, sesame seeds, pumpkin seeds, flaxseed, and kosher salt in a large bowl. Add the water mixture and stir together until combined.

2. Cover with a kitchen towel and let rest at room temperature for 1 hour.

3. Prepare two medium baking sheets with parchment paper. Preheat the oven to 350°F. Split the batter between both sheets and spread into a thin layer. Bake in the oven for 10 minutes.

4. Remove from the oven and cut the dough into 15 rectangle portions per set. Place back in the oven and bake for another 40 to 50 minutes, or until the edges are light brown and crispy.

5. Take the crackers out of the oven and allow to cool slightly until you can handle them. Separate any pieces that are still attached to each other, and place on a wire rack to cool completely. They can be stored at room temperature in an airtight container for 1 week.

CHEWCATCH

With their boots always breaking new snow, the Banuk require hearty food that travels well. That's why they came up with Chewcatch—this fish jerky is easy to carry and can last weeks in the frigid cold of the Cut. The prep can take some time, and eating it can be quite the exercise for one's jaw, but that's not so much a concern for these hardened survivalist types.

DIFFICULTY: ◆◆◆◇◇

PREP: 30 minutes **INACTIVE TIME:** 12 hours **COOK TIME:** 5 hours
YIELD: 2 pounds of jerky **DIETARY NOTES:** Dairy-Free

2 cups soy sauce
1 tablespoon light brown sugar
2 tablespoons honey
½ teaspoon liquid smoke
1 tablespoon white miso
2 teaspoons ginger powder
1 teaspoon garlic powder
½ teaspoon ground black pepper
2 pounds salmon, skin on

1. Combine the soy sauce, brown sugar, honey, liquid smoke, miso, ginger powder, garlic powder, and pepper in a gallon-size sealable bag. Cut the salmon ⅛ to ¼ inch thick, keeping the skin on. Add the salmon to the bag and toss to coat. Place in the refrigerator overnight to marinate, up to 24 hours.

NOTE: *Make sure your knife is extremely sharp. This will make cutting the salmon much easier.*

2. Preheat the oven to 175°F. Prepare a baking sheet with aluminum foil, place a wire rack on top, and top with parchment paper. Take the fish out of the marinade and let excess liquid drip off. Place on the parchment paper.

3. Bake in the oven for 4 to 5 hours, or until the salmon is dry and chewy. Let cool completely. Store in an airtight container in the refrigerator for up to 2 weeks.

NOTE: *The jerky can be enjoyed with the skin on, or you can remove it after the jerky has baked.*

CUTFISH CAKES

The Banuk live in incredibly small, nomadic groups without getting sick of one another, somehow. After a successful bout of ice fishing, the members of these "weraks" will often combine their catch in the form of Cutfish Cakes. They mince the fish, mixing it with all manner of seasoning, salt, and breadcrumbs, then divide the mixture into mostly equal-sized patties—a larger patty is reserved for the chieftain.

DIFFICULTY: ◆◆◇◇◇

PREP: 30 minutes   **INACTIVE TIME:** 1 hour   **COOK TIME:** 15 minutes   **YIELD:** 8 fish cakes   **DIETARY NOTES:** Gluten-Free

FISKEFRIKADELLER

1¼ pounds cod
½ onion, quartered
¼ ounce fresh dill
¼ cup parsley
1 egg
⅓ cup panko
1 teaspoon garlic powder
3 tablespoons potato starch
1 teaspoon kosher salt
½ teaspoon ground black pepper
1 teaspoon vegetable oil

RÉMOULADE

⅓ cup mayo
3 tablespoons sour cream
1 tablespoon Dijon mustard
1 tablespoon capers, minced
2 tablespoons pickles, minced
2 tablespoons lemon juice
Kosher salt, to taste
Ground black pepper, to taste

TO MAKE THE FISKEFRIKADELLER:

1. Place the cod in a food processor and pulse until the fish is chopped finely. Transfer to a large bowl. Place the onion, dill, and parsley in the food processor and pulse until finely chopped, then transfer to the bowl with the cod. Add the egg, panko, garlic powder, potato starch, salt, and pepper to the bowl. Mix until everything just comes together.

2. Cover and place in the refrigerator to rest for 30 minutes. Split the mixture into eight equal pieces and form into patties. Place on a plate, cover, and refrigerate for another 30 minutes.

3. Heat a medium nonstick pan with the vegetable oil over medium-high heat. Place four of the prepared patties in the pan. Cook until the first side is golden brown, about 5 minutes. Flip and cook until the other side is golden brown, about 5 minutes. Add 2 tablespoons of water to the pan and cover. Steam the patties until cooked through. Repeat with the remaining patties.

TO MAKE THE RÉMOULADE:

4. Combine the rémoulade ingredients in an airtight container. Cover and store until needed. Can be stored in the refrigerator for about 1 week.

FROST-THAW SOUP

The Cut's frosty winds could freeze the Blaze Sac off a Bellowback. And so, a good Banuk dish is expected to warm one's spirits as much as it fills one's gut. This creamy fish soup takes advantage of the abundance of freshwater fish found in the region's fast-flowing mountain streams. This recipe's simple as its name, and a hot bowlful promises to keep winter at bay!

DIFFICULTY: ◆◆◇◇◇

PREP: 30 minutes **COOK TIME:** 30 minutes **YIELD:** 4 servings **DIETARY NOTES:** Gluten-Free

3 tablespoons unsalted butter
½ onion, chopped
Kosher salt, to taste
Ground black pepper, to taste
3 garlic cloves, minced
2 celery stalks, chopped
1 fennel bulb, chopped
1 carrot, chopped
4 cups fish stock
1 parsnip, chopped into large pieces
1 russet potato, chopped into large pieces
1 pound steelhead trout
1 cup milk
1 cup heavy cream
1/2 ounce fresh dill, chopped
Juice of 1 lemon

1. Place a large pot with the butter over medium-low heat. Once the butter has melted, add the onions and sauté until they become translucent, about 5 minutes. Season with salt and pepper. Add the garlic, celery, fennel, and carrot. Cook for about 7 minutes, until the carrot has softened slightly.

2. Add the fish stock, parsnip, and potato. Bring to a simmer, reduce the heat, and cook for 15 to 20 minutes, until the potato is tender.

3. Add the trout and cook until just cooked through, about 5 to 8 minutes.

4. Add the milk, heavy cream, dill, and lemon juice. Mix until well combined and heated through. Season with salt and pepper.

BLUE LIGHT PUDDING

This warm rice pudding is named for both the blue skybrush on top and the blue machine light which Banuk shamans revere, and you can taste why! After our frost-fingered ascent to Song's Edge, a couple bowls of this stuff put the fire back in our coals like nothing else. It feels soft, nurturing, and sweet—hard to believe it's a product of the grizzled Banuk! But I guess everyone's got their soft side, even if it needs to thaw out a bit.

DIFFICULTY: ◆◆◇◇◇

PREP: 15 minutes **COOK TIME:** 40 minutes **YIELD:** 4 servings **DIETARY NOTES:** Vegan, Gluten-Free

1½ cups water
½ teaspoon kosher salt
1 cinnamon stick
¾ cup arborio rice
3 cups almond milk
2 tablespoons sugar
2 tablespoons maple syrup
½ vanilla bean,
   seeds scraped and pod discarded
Ground cinnamon, for garnish
Blueberries, for garnish

1. Combine the water, salt, cinnamon stick, and arborio rice in a medium pot. Heat over medium-high heat and bring to a boil. Reduce the heat to medium-low and simmer until the water has been absorbed, about 10 minutes.

2. Remove and discard the cinnamon stick. Add ½ cup almond milk, along with the sugar, maple syrup, and vanilla bean seeds. Mix and continue to heat until the milk has been absorbed, about 5 minutes. Keep adding ½ cup of almond milk at a time and stirring, until 3 cups of milk have been added and absorbed in total. This should take about 30 minutes. The rice should be extremely tender after the cooking time is done.

3. Split into four bowls, and top with ground cinnamon and fresh blueberries.

QUEN

— A LETTER TO THE CLAIM —

Journal, I know it's been a while. A lot has happened. But I have fantastic news.
    Earlier today, I was minding The Frostclaw's Head—that's my very own kitchen. All mine. The Banuk let me keep the machine's skull as a trophy. Most of the soot came off easily enough. You should see when parents bring their little sparks in for their birthdays—their eyes widen with wonder. And the food is a hit. I'm in the kitchen every day, and I couldn't be happier.
    At least, I thought I couldn't be happier.
    A courier arrived holding a bundle of fine foreign parchment bound in an odd, ornate, orange-and-green ribbon. He said it'd been handed over at a recent embassy and passed along, and now it's here. Suffice to say, I think the wilds of the West may be calling me back…

Milduf of Mainspring,

My name's Kari. I'm writing on behalf of your friend, Pentalla. She says she hopes you have not been captured, maimed, or killed recently.

Your friend and I ran into one another in the wilds. I'm just a cook from a tribe called the Quen.

Pentalla seemed very determined for me to note down some of my recipes for you. So determined, in fact, that when I refused, she turned her spear on me and said, "Write."

So here I am . . . writing!

I've enclosed the recipes, as she requested. She has also asked I mention you are welcome to visit her at the Grove. She is teaching there. (Obviously not diplomacy.)

If you visit, I hope she'll offer you a kinder welcome than she did me. She really comes on strong.

Oh, she also wants me to mention that she "passed by Chainscrape on her way back and sorted things out but is now banned for life"—I don't know what that means, but I sure hope she was merciful.

She said she was going to let me go . . . You know, I survived a shipwreck? And now this??

As I said, I'm just a cook. I don't handle heat well outside of a kitchen.

RUBY SUNRISE

Guess I should start with the basics. This is a simple meal that we often prepare for low-ranking members of our fleet. Soldiers, workers, deckhands. We simmer eggs in tomatoes and herbs. It's a real crowd-pleaser . . . unless that particular crowd doesn't like anchovy.

DIFFICULTY: ◆◆◇◇◇

PREP TIME: 30 minutes **COOK TIME:** 45 minutes **YIELD:** 2 servings **DIETARY NOTES:** Dairy-Free

2 tablespoons olive oil
½ onion, thinly sliced
½ red bell pepper, thinly sliced
½ yellow bell pepper, thinly sliced
4 garlic cloves, chopped
2 teaspoons whole cumin seeds, lightly crushed
2 tablespoons anchovy paste
One 28-ounce can crushed tomatoes
2 teaspoons smoked paprika
1 teaspoon ground coriander
1 teaspoon sugar
4 eggs
6 sprigs cilantro
2 scallions, chopped
Slices of crusty bread, for serving

1. Heat a medium stainless-steel pan over medium-high heat. Add the olive oil and allow to heat for 30 seconds. Add the onion and cook until softened, about 3 minutes.

2. Add the bell peppers and cook until golden, about 10 to 12 minutes. Add the garlic and cumin seeds and cook until fragrant, about 1 minute.

3. Add the anchovy paste, crushed tomatoes, smoked paprika, coriander, and sugar. Mix until well combined. Reduce the heat to medium, cover, and simmer for 15 to 20 minutes, or until the mixture thickens. Make sure to mix together a few times to prevent it from sticking.

4. Create a small divot and crack an egg into it. Repeat with the remaining eggs. Cover again and cook for 5 to 8 minutes, until the eggs set. Remove from the heat and top with cilantro and scallions. Serve with slices of bread.

155

SALTY PLANKS

I know the name sounds woody, and dry—this dish is anything but. We slice the pepper and cured fish into "planks." I'm sure your blade-wielding friend here will be great at that part. After that, it's all about balancing the flavors.

DIFFICULTY: ◆◆◇◇◇

PREP TIME: 45 minutes **INACTIVE TIME:** 2 hours **COOK TIME:** 25 minutes
YIELD: 4 to 6 servings **DIETARY NOTES:** Dairy-Free

ROAST BELL PEPPER
3 red bell peppers, cored and cut in half
1 tablespoon olive oil
¼ teaspoon kosher salt
¼ teaspoon ground black pepper

DRESSING
Juice and zest of 1 orange
¼ cup olive oil

FOR ASSEMBLY
2 salted cod fillets
2 garlic cloves, sliced
½ cup kalamata olives, pits removed

1. Prepare the salted cod by rinsing off the salt. Place in an airtight bowl and fill with water. Cover and place in the refrigerator for 30 minutes. Drain, rinse, and place back in the bowl. Fill with water, cover, and place in the refrigerator for another 30 minutes. Repeat twice more, or until the cod is no longer super salty. Set aside in the refrigerator until you are ready to assemble the salad.

2. Preheat the oven to 425°F. Line a baking sheet with parchment paper and place the bell peppers, skin side up, on the tray. Brush with olive oil, then generously season with salt and pepper. Bake in the oven for 20 to 25 minutes, until the bell peppers begin to char.

3. Remove from the oven and allow to cool completely. Remove and discard the bell pepper skins. Set aside until you are ready to assemble.

4. Whisk together the ingredients for the dressing. Can be stored in an airtight container in the refrigerator until you are ready to assemble.

5. To assemble, cut the roast bell pepper into thick slices. Split between your serving plates and top with the garlic and kalamata olives.

6. Remove the cod from the water and thoroughly pat dry. Cut into small bite-size pieces and place on top of the serving plates. Drizzle a generous helping of the dressing over each serving.

CRAB HOT POT

It was a real luxury to cook this for my comrades at Legacy's Landfall. We had lost so much in the shipwreck, and this new land was challenging. But after we caught enough shellfish, and poured the first bowls of this, many of us felt that the worst of the tragedy was behind us. It tasted like a bit of home.

DIFFICULTY: ◆◆◆◇◇

PREP TIME: 45 minutes **INACTIVE TIME:** 3 hours **COOK TIME:** 1 hour
YIELD: 4 servings **DIETARY NOTES:** Dairy-Free, Alcohol

BROTH
- 1 kombu
- 1 cup niboshi, heads and guts removed
- 6 cups water
- 1 garlic bulb, cut in half
- 1 onion, quartered
- One 4-inch piece ginger, sliced
- 1 cup bonito flakes

HOT POT
- 3 tablespoons sake
- 2 tablespoons soy sauce
- 1 tablespoon mirin
- 1 tablespoon sugar
- ⅓ cup white miso
- 1 carrot, peeled and cut into bite-size pieces
- ¼ napa cabbage, sliced thick
- 3 negi, cut into thick slices
- 8 ounces extra firm tofu, cut into large portions
- 4 shiitake mushrooms, stems removed
- 1 bunch shimeji mushrooms
- 1 pound snow crab legs
- 1 bunch enoki mushrooms
- 1 serving udon, per person

TO MAKE THE BROTH:

1. Place the kombu, niboshi, and water in a medium pot and cover. Let rest for 3 hours. Place the pot, uncovered, over medium heat. Right before the water comes to a boil, remove and discard the kombu.

2. Add the garlic, onion, and ginger to the pot over medium-high heat. Bring to a boil, then reduce the heat and simmer for 20 minutes. Add the bonito flakes and simmer for another 10 minutes. Strain through a fine-mesh strainer and discard all the ingredients, keeping only the broth. Set the broth aside, or allow to cool completely before storing in an airtight container and refrigerating. Can keep in the refrigerator for up to 5 days.

TO MAKE THE HOT POT:

3. Whisk together the sake, soy sauce, mirin, sugar, and miso in a small bowl. Heat the broth in a large pot over medium-high heat. Reduce the heat to a simmer and add the carrot. Cook for 10 minutes.

4. Add the cabbage, negi, and tofu. Simmer for about 5 minutes. Pour in the soy sauce mixture and gently mix in. Add the shiitake mushrooms and shimeji mushrooms and cook until the mushrooms begin to soften, about 5 minutes.

5. Add the crab legs and cook until heated and cooked through, about 5 minutes.

6. Finally, add the enoki mushrooms. Cook for another 2 minutes. Serve with cooked udon.

DELTA DUMPLINGS

I can't think of a more joyful thing to eat than a dumpling. From the outside, it's hard to tell what each one contains, giving the dish an element of surprise. Below, I've listed my favorite fillings, though back in the Delta, there are more types of dumplings than one can imagine. If only I had been as prepared to be surprised by your friend while I was foraging . . .

DIFFICULTY: ◆◆◆◇◇

PREP TIME: 1½ hours   INACTIVE TIME: 30 minutes   COOK TIME: 10 minutes
YIELD: 60 dumplings   DIETARY NOTES: Dairy-Free

DUMPLINGS

14 ounces napa cabbage, thinly sliced
3 teaspoons kosher salt
1 pound ground pork
½ pound scallops, chopped
¼ cup water chestnuts, minced
1 tablespoon ginger, minced
4 scallions, diced
1 tablespoon sesame oil
2 teaspoons soy sauce
1 teaspoon sake
1 teaspoon sugar
60 round gyoza wrappers
Canola oil, for the pan

TO MAKE THE DUMPLINGS:

1. Place the sliced cabbage and 2 teaspoons of salt in a strainer over a bowl and allow to sit for at least 15 minutes to remove excess water from the cabbage. Squeeze the cabbage to further remove excess water.

2. Combine the cabbage, ground pork, scallops, water chestnuts, ginger, and scallions in a medium bowl. Add the sesame oil, soy sauce, sake, the remaining 1 teaspoon salt, and sugar. Mix together.

3. Place a small bowl of water next to the area where you will be making the dumplings. Take a gyoza wrapper and place 1 to 2 teaspoons of the filling in the center. Wet your index finger and use that to wet the edges of the wrapper.

4. Fold the wrapper in half and pinch the center together. Pleat one side of the wrapper, then the other side, until the dumpling is completely sealed. Repeat with the remaining wrappers.

SAUCE

3 tablespoons soy sauce
2 tablespoons black vinegar
1 tablespoon chile oil
2 teaspoons sugar
1 teaspoon sesame oil
1 teaspoon sesame seeds
1 scallion, chopped

5. If planning to store the dumplings frozen, place on a baking sheet with parchment paper and cover with plastic wrap. Set in the freezer for at least 30 minutes, then put all the dumplings in a sealable bag. The dumplings can be stored in the freezer for up to 2 months. When cooking the frozen dumplings, do not thaw them first.

6. To cook fresh dumplings, heat a large pan over medium-high heat with canola oil. Add a single layer of dumplings and cook until the bottoms brown slightly, about 1 to 2 minutes (3 to 4 minutes if frozen).

7. Add ½ cup of water and cover with a lid. Let the dumplings steam until the water has completely evaporated and the bottoms have crisped up slightly.

8. Repeat Steps 6 and 7 with more dumplings until the desired amount has been cooked. Serve immediately.

TO MAKE THE SAUCE:

9. Whisk all of the sauce ingredients together to combine. Can be stored in an airtight container in the refrigerator for up to 1 week.

MARINE'S ARROW

We Quen spend much of our time on the high seas. Sometimes we don't dock for weeks or months. And so we must supplement our dry food stocks by catching fresh fish and preparing it right on the deck. This recipe is a simple skewer, best prepared with semi-mild ocean fish.

DIFFICULTY: ◆◆◇◇◇

PREP TIME: 30 minutes   **INACTIVE TIME:** 30 minutes   **COOK TIME:** 12 minutes
YIELD: 4 skewers   **DIETARY NOTES:** Dairy-Free, Gluten-Free

1 pound mahi-mahi, cut into bite-size pieces
¼ cup lime juice
¼ cup white vinegar
⅓ cup vegetable oil
1 tablespoon ancho chile powder
1 teaspoon paprika
½ teaspoon ground cumin
5 garlic cloves, minced
1 orange bell pepper, cut into bite-size pieces
½ red onion, cut into bite-size pieces
4 wooden skewers

EQUIPMENT
Grill

1. Put the mahi-mahi, lime juice, white vinegar, vegetable oil, chile powder, paprika, cumin, and garlic in an airtight bag and shake until the fish is coated. Place in the refrigerator and marinate for 30 minutes, no more than 1 hour. After marination is complete, reserve the marinade.

2. Allow the wooden skewers to soak in water for 30 minutes prior to grilling.

3. With a wooden skewer, pierce a piece of bell pepper, followed by a piece of red onion, then a piece of mahi-mahi. Add another piece of red onion and another of mahi-mahi. Repeat this sequence to finish up the skewer.

4. Repeat Step 3 with the remaining wooden skewers. Preheat the grill.

5. Right before you put the skewers on the grill, brush each with the fish marinade.

6. Grill the skewers for 8 to 12 minutes over the hot side of the grill, flipping to crisp all sides.

CEO'S BANQUET

This isn't so much a dish as a feast. In spite of our issues acquiring resources after landing, our esteemed Ceo demanded this banquet be prepared for him every night. And so we searched frantically—Shrimp! Mussels! Clams!—to please him. As I held the burden of preparing the dish to his very specific tastes, I could sample a bite here or there, and I can tell you the effort was worth it.

<u>Important:</u> Be sure to discard any unopened clam or mussel shells—I shudder to think of the punishment that awaits the cook who poisons the Ceo.

DIFFICULTY: ◆◆◆◆◆

PREP TIME: 45 minutes   **COOK TIME:** 45 minutes   **YIELD:** 4 servings   **DIETARY NOTES:** Dairy-Free

SHRIMP STOCK

½ pound shrimp, heads and peels on
1 tablespoon canola oil
½ teaspoon saffron threads
1 leek, cut into large chunks
1 fennel bulb, quartered
3 sprigs thyme
1 bay leaf
1 tablespoon black peppercorns
4 cups vegetable broth

TO MAKE THE SHRIMP STOCK:

1. Remove the heads and peels from the shrimp and set those on the side. Finish cleaning the shrimp by removing and discarding the veins. Rinse the shrimp and place in an airtight container in the refrigerator until needed for the paella.

2. Heat a medium pot with the canola oil over medium-high heat. Add the shrimp heads and peels. Cook until the shrimp heads are seared, about 3 to 5 minutes. Add the remaining ingredients and bring to a boil.

3. Reduce the heat to low and allow to simmer for 20 minutes. Afterward, transfer to a bowl with a mesh strainer, discarding all the bits. The stock can be stored in an airtight container in the refrigerator for up to 2 days.

167

PAELLA

1 tablespoon canola oil
1 onion, chopped
1 red bell pepper, chopped
6 garlic cloves, chopped
1 large tomato, chopped
2 teaspoons sweet paprika
1 cup bomba rice
2½ cups shrimp stock
Shrimp (from the stock)
8 mussels
8 littleneck clams
1 lemon, cut into wedges, for garnish
2 tablespoons parsley, for garnish

EQUIPMENT
Medium paella pan

TO MAKE THE PAELLA:

4. Heat the canola oil in a medium paella pan over medium-high heat. Add the onion and bell pepper and cook until softened and brown, about 10 to 15 minutes.

5. Add the garlic and cook for another 2 minutes. Add the tomato and paprika and cook until the tomato has softened and the liquid has evaporated, about 5 minutes.

6. Add the bomba rice, stir in with the other ingredients, and cook for 2 minutes. Then, add the shrimp stock and give the pan a good shake to level everything out. Bring the stock to a boil and reduce the heat to medium, maintaining a light boil. Cook until about 75% of the liquid has evaporated, about 10 minutes.

7. Add the shrimp, mussels, and clams by placing them slightly in the rice. Cook for 5 to 8 more minutes, until there is no liquid and the rice begins to smell slightly toasty.

8. Turn off the heat, cover the pan, and let sit for 10 minutes. Uncover and check that all the clams and mussels have opened—discard any unopened shells, as they are not safe to eat. Garnish with lemon wedges and parsley.

IMPERIAL DARK SEAFOAM

As the chosen people, we are fortunate to have inherited culinary traditions from the Ancestors, and so we know this green fruit was coveted before the Time of Ashes. Supposedly, many forewent even a roof over their heads to delight in its rich flesh. I hope that by sharing this most precious of recipes, my life will be spared. However, I warn that this dish may prove impossible to make, as it also involves acquiring "chocolate"—an extremely rare confection reserved for the Imperial family.

DIFFICULTY: ◆◇◇◇◇

PREP TIME: 30 minutes **INACTIVE TIME:** 1 hour **YIELD:** 3 to 4 servings **DIETARY NOTES:** Vegan, Gluten-Free

10 ounces avocado
4 ounces dairy-free dark chocolate, melted and cooled
⅓ cup maple syrup
2 tablespoons coconut sugar
3 tablespoons cocoa powder
½ cup coconut milk
1 teaspoon kosher salt
Coconut Whipped Cream (page 75), for topping

1. Place all the ingredients in a food processor. Pulse until everything is well combined and the mixture is slightly fluffy. Split the mixture between 3 to 4 serving bowls, then cover with plastic wrap and allow to rest in the refrigerator for at least 1 hour, up to 4 days.

2. Serve with coconut whipped cream.

POTIONS

No traveling cook who wishes to survive the wilds should be without potions. From east to west, wonderful concoctions are being produced to boost healing, stamina, and protection against corruption or elements. Amazingly, each of the following potions tastes great as well!

HEALTH POTION

This is a top seller. No hunter ventures into the wilds without it. You'll often see them guzzling this stuff down in the heat of battle. I don't know how they manage to down a bottle after being flung across a field by a Thunderjaw's tail, but I also don't understand a lot of what makes those danger-loving types tick.

DIFFICULTY: ◆ ◆ ◆ ◇ ◇

PREP TIME: 45 minutes   **INACTIVE TIME:** 5 hours   **COOK TIME:** 3 hours
YIELD: 8 to 12 servings of broth   **DIETARY NOTES:** Dairy-Free, Gluten-Free, Alcohol

BONE BROTH

2 pounds chicken backs

2 lemongrass stalks, smashed

One 3-inch piece ginger, sliced

One 1-inch piece galangal, sliced

1 shallot, quartered

1 tablespoon whole black
    peppercorns

2 teaspoons coriander seeds

1 pod black cardamom

½ cinnamon stick

8 cups water,
    plus more for cleaning

4 scallions

½ bunch cilantro

HEALTH POTION (PER SERVING)

Ice, plus more for serving

1 tablespoon Lemongrass Syrup
    (page 187)

4 ounces bone broth

1½ ounces bourbon

1 ounce lime juice

Pinch of kosher salt

Cilantro sprigs, for garnish

EQUIPMENT

Cocktail shaker

TO MAKE THE BONE BROTH:

1. Place the chicken backs in a large bowl. Cover with water and let sit for 15 minutes. Drain and rinse off each piece. Transfer to a stockpot and fill with enough water to cover the meat. Bring to a boil over high heat and allow to boil for 5 minutes. Strain and rinse all of the meat, removing any scum. Transfer to a clean stockpot.

2. Add the lemongrass, ginger, galangal, shallot, black peppercorns, coriander seeds, black cardamom, and cinnamon stick. Add the 8 cups of water and bring to a boil over medium-high heat. Reduce the heat to medium-low and simmer for 2 hours.

3. Add the scallions and cilantro and simmer for another 1 hour.

4. After the broth is finished simmering, carefully strain the pot into another container to separate the broth from all the ingredients. Allow to cool, then place in the refrigerator for at least 5 hours before making the health potions. Can be stored in an airtight container in the refrigerator for up to 5 days.

TO MAKE THE HEALTH POTION:

5. Fill a cocktail shaker with ice. Add the lemongrass syrup, bone broth, bourbon, lime juice, and salt. Cover and shake for 20 seconds. Taste and flavor with additional salt if needed.

6. Prepare a glass with ice and cilantro sprigs. Pour in the shaken cocktail.

STAMINA POTION

Nothing can revive stamina quite like a good night's sleep, but now that I've voyaged through treacherous plains, I know that that's not always an option. Quaffing down just one mug of this hearty concoction comes a close second to shut-eye when it comes to revitalization.

DIFFICULTY: ◆◆◆◇◇

PREP TIME: 15 minutes **INACTIVE TIME:** 12 hours **COOK TIME:** 30 minutes
YIELD: 10 servings of syrup **DIETARY NOTES:** Vegan, Gluten-Free

PASSION FRUIT SYRUP
½ cup sugar
½ cup water
3 passion fruit, pulp only

STAMINA POTION (PER SERVING)
1 tablespoon gyokuro tea leaves
1 tablespoon goji berries
2 slices orange
1 to 2 tablespoons passion fruit syrup
1 cup hot water, 140°F

TO MAKE THE PASSION FRUIT SYRUP:

1. Whisk the sugar and water together in a small saucepan and place over medium-high heat. Once the sugar dissolves, add the passion fruit pulp and bring to a simmer. Reduce the heat to medium-low and simmer for 25 minutes.

2. Strain into an airtight container and allow to cool to room temperature. Store in the refrigerator for at least 12 hours, up to 2 weeks.

TO MAKE THE STAMINA POTION:

3. Place the gyokuro, goji berries, orange slices, and passion fruit syrup in a small teapot. Add the hot water and steep for 90 seconds.

4. Strain into a mug and serve.

CLEANSE POTION

Whether it's a spray of machine acid, a bite of frost, or a night on the ales they're looking to recover from, my clientele never look past a cleanse potion. This delicious blend of fruits, greens, and fermented milk does the trick every time. Its purifying properties are simply indisputable.

DIFFICULTY: ◆ ◆ ◇ ◇ ◇

PREP TIME: 15 minutes   **YIELD:** 2 servings   **DIETARY NOTES:** Gluten-Free

1 banana
½ cup spinach
2 kale leaves, ribs removed
1 celery stalk
½ small Granny Smith apple
½ cup pineapple
½ seedless cucumber, peeled
Juice of ½ lemon
½ cup Greek yogurt
½ cup coconut milk

EQUIPMENT
Blender

1. Place all the ingredients in a blender and blend until smooth. Split between 2 glasses and serve immediately.

ANTIDOTE

My pa always said, "The best way to get healthy is to not get sick at all"—pretty useless advice unless you've got this potion handy. It packs a hefty serving of corruption glaze root, so no matter what its drinker comes up against, they'll remain free from whatever toxins they might come afoul of in the wilds. I'm always sure to wait for the drink to cool before whisking in the final ingredients.

DIFFICULTY: ◆◆◇◇◇

PREP TIME: 45 minutes **INACTIVE TIME:** 3 hours **COOK TIME:** 30 minutes
YIELD: 4 servings of lemonade **DIETARY NOTES:** Vegetarian, Gluten-Free, Dairy-Free

GINGER LEMONADE
2½ to 3½ cups water
2 tablespoons sugar
⅓ cup honey
One 4-inch piece ginger, sliced
1 cup lemon juice
  (about 5 to 6 lemons)

ANTIDOTE (PER SERVING)
1 cup ginger lemonade
½ teaspoon matcha
½ cup ginger beer

TO MAKE THE GINGER LEMONADE:

1. Start with the simple syrup. Combine ½ cup water with the sugar, honey, and ginger slices in a medium saucepan and place over medium-high heat. Whisk until the sugar dissolves, then bring to a boil. Reduce the heat and simmer for 10 minutes. Remove the syrup from the heat and let sit for 30 minutes to cool and to let the ginger steep.

2. In a pitcher, combine the simple syrup (remove and discard the ginger), lemon juice, and the remaining 2 to 3 cups of water. Mix together. Store in the refrigerator for at least 3 hours before serving. Can keep in the refrigerator for up to 7 days.

TO MAKE THE ANTIDOTE:

3. Sift the matcha into a bowl. Pour ¼ cup of the ginger lemonade in and whisk the matcha until completely smooth. Combine the rest of the lemonade with the matcha mixture, then transfer to a large glass. Add the ginger beer and serve immediately.

OVERDRAW POTION

Hunters who make regular use of a bow will appreciate the energy boost an overdraw potion provides. The sudden burst of energy allows them to achieve a tighter draw and more powerful hit. I'll sip one of these if I see a large group is being seated, knowing I'm going to be sweating it out getting their food to them. Get's me bouncing like a Leaplasher every time.

DIFFICULTY: ◆♢♢♢♢

PREP TIME: 15 minutes   YIELD: 1 drink   DIETARY NOTES: Vegan, Gluten-Free

2 sprigs mint, plus more for serving
Ice
Juice of ½ blood orange
Juice of 1 lime
½ ounce simple syrup
Crushed ice, for serving
½ cup club soda

EQUIPMENT
Cocktail shaker

1. Muddle the mint in a cocktail shaker. Add the ice, blood orange juice, lime juice, and simple syrup. Cover and shake for 10 seconds.
2. Prepare a glass with fresh mint and crushed ice. Pour the shaken cocktail into the glass and top with club soda.

RESIST FIRE POTION

Razor-clawed machines are fearsome enough without throwing fire into the mix. I tell any hunter to stock up on this potion before facing anything that's got a canister of Blaze strapped to its back. The smart ones listen.

DIFFICULTY: ◆◆◇◇◇

PREP TIME: 20 minutes **INACTIVE TIME:** 8 hours **COOK TIME:** 30 minutes
YIELD: 6 to 8 servings **DIETARY NOTES:** Vegan, Gluten-Free

ORANGE SYRUP

Peels from 2 oranges
3 pods green cardamom
¾ cup sugar
1 cup orange juice
4 sprigs mint

RESIST FIRE POTION

6 cups water
5 Earl Grey tea bags
Orange syrup
Ice, for serving
Fresh orange slices, for serving

TO MAKE THE ORANGE SYRUP:

1. Combine the orange peels, cardamom, sugar, and orange juice in a medium saucepan. Bring to a boil, then lower the heat to low and allow to simmer for 10 minutes. Cover and remove from heat. Add the mint and steep for 45 minutes.

2. Strain through a mesh strainer into a large pitcher.

TO MAKE THE RESIST FIRE POTION:

3. Heat water in a large pot over medium-high heat until boiling. Add the tea bags. Turn off the heat and steep for 5 minutes. Remove the tea bags, transfer to the pitcher with the orange syrup, and stir together.

4. Allow the mixture to cool completely, then store in the refrigerator overnight before serving. Serve in a glass with ice and fresh orange slices.

RESIST FREEZE POTION

Would've loved one of these while I was shivering my way through the Cut. This sweet "blue tea" is a great way to counter a cold blast. The only downside is it takes a good 12 hours for the syrup to settle into its full vigor, so I try to prep more than I need to keep the Frostclaw's Head well-stocked.

DIFFICULTY: ◆◇◇◇◇

PREP TIME: 15 minutes **INACTIVE TIME:** 12 hours **COOK TIME:** 10 minutes
YIELD: 10 servings of syrup **DIETARY NOTES:** Vegetarian, Gluten-Free, Dairy-Free

LEMONGRASS SYRUP

¼ cup sugar
½ cup honey
½ cup water
2 lemongrass stalks, smashed

RESIST FREEZE POTION (PER SERVING)

10 dried butterfly pea flowers
2 slices ginger
1 teaspoon dried lemongrass
2 to 3 tablespoons lemongrass syrup
1 cup boiling water

TO MAKE THE LEMONGRASS SYRUP:

1. Whisk together the sugar, honey, and water in a saucepan and place over medium-high heat. Once the sugar dissolves, add the lemongrass and bring to a simmer. Reduce the heat to medium-low and simmer for 10 minutes. Then remove from the heat, cover, and steep for 20 minutes.

2. Transfer into an airtight container. Allow to cool to room temperature. Store in the refrigerator for at least 12 hours, up to 2 weeks.

TO MAKE THE RESIST FREEZE POTION:

3. Place the butterfly pea flowers, ginger slices, dried lemongrass, and lemongrass syrup in a small teapot. Add the hot water and steep for 6 minutes.

4. Strain into a mug and serve.

CONVERSION CHARTS

VOLUME

U.S.	METRIC
⅕ teaspoon	1 ml
1 teaspoon	5 ml
1 tablespoon	15 ml
1 fluid ounce	30 ml
⅕ cup	50 ml
¼ cup	60 ml
⅓ cup	80 ml
3.4 fluid ounces	100 ml
½ cup	120 ml
⅔ cup	160 ml
¾ cup	180 ml
1 cup	240 ml
1 pint (2 cups)	480 ml
1 quart (4 cups)	.95 liter

WEIGHT

U.S.	METRIC
0.5 ounce	14 grams
1 ounce	28 grams
¼ pound	113 grams
⅓ pound	151 grams
½ pound	227 grams
1 pound	454 grams

TEMPERATURES

FAHRENHEIT	CELSIUS
200°	93°
212°	100°
250°	120°
275°	135°
300°	150°
325°	165°
350°	177°
400°	205°
425°	220°
450°	233°
475°	245°
500°	260°

DIETARY CONSIDERATIONS

DIETARY AND PERSONAL RESTRICTIONS
Cooking is always a personal experience, and you should always feel comfortable replacing or removing any ingredients that you and your guests don't normally eat, for either personal or dietary reasons. Although you have a full experience of knowing what type of ingredients to avoid or replace, here are a few suggestions for some general dietary needs.

ADAPTING TO VEGETARIAN DIETS
Several recipes in this book are vegetarian- or vegan-friendly. Many recipes can be adapted to your dietary needs. Replace meat broths/stocks with vegetable broths/stocks. Swap out proteins with your favorite grilled vegetables or meat substitutes. This will affect cooking times, so plan ahead.

ADAPTING TO GLUTEN-FREE DIETS
For most recipes, you can use equal rations of a gluten substitute for flour, but be prepared to modify the quantity just in case the consistency seems off compared to how it is described in the recipes.

ADAPTING TO LACTOSE-FREE DIETS
Feel free to replace milk and heavy cream with your favorite nondairy milk. There are also plenty of alternatives to replace butter in recipes. It is not normally suggested to replace butter with oil, because it doesn't give the same consistency needed for certain recipes. If you do use oil instead, approach it in smaller batches.

ABOUT THE AUTHORS

VICTORIA ROSENTHAL launched her blog, *Pixelated Provisions*, in 2012 to combine her passion for video games and food by re-creating consumables found in her favorite games. Victoria has authored *Fallout: The Vault Dweller's Official Cookbook*, *Destiny: The Official Cookbook*, *Street Fighter: The Official Street Food Cookbook*, and *The Ultimate FINAL FANTASY XIV Cookbook*. Feel free to say hello on social media at @PixelatedVicka.

RICK BARBA is one of the most published book authors in the video game industry, with more than 130 game-related titles in print, including *Diablo III: The Official Limited Edition Strategy Guide* and the novel *XCOM 2: Escalation* (Insight Editions, 2017). A graduate of the Iowa Writers' Workshop, Rick has been on the writing faculty at Santa Clara University and the University of Nebraska Omaha, and has published fiction in numerous literary journals such as *Chicago Review*, *Black Warrior Review*, *AQR*, and Gordon Lish's *The Quarterly*. He's thrilled that the content of his two Starfleet Academy novels (*The Delta Anomaly* and *The Gemini Agent*) is part of the official Star Trek canon. Rick lives just outside Boulder, Colorado.

GUERRILLA NARRATIVE TEAM: Story by Emil Cholich. Editorial support from Annie Kitain and Sadie Smiles.

PO Box 3088
San Rafael, CA 94912
www.insighteditions.com

Find us on Facebook: www.facebook.com/InsightEditions
Follow us on Instagram: @insighteditions

©2024 Sony Interactive Entertainment Europe. Horizon Forbidden West is a trademark of Sony Interactive Entertainment LLC. "PlayStation Family Mark" is a registered trademark of Sony Interactive Entertainment, Inc.

All rights reserved. Published by Insight Editions, San Rafael, California, in 2024.
No part of this book may be reproduced in any form without written permission from the publisher.
Library of Congress Cataloging-in-Publication Data available.
ISBN: 979-8-88663-310-8

Special thanks to: Claudia Gibbardo, Chanté Goodman, Ilya Golitsyn, Madse Krivokutya, Sunjeev Kumar, Ben McCaw, Craig Stuart, Jessica Williams, and the entire team at Guerrilla

Publisher: Raoul Goff
VP, Co-Publisher: Vanessa Lopez
VP, Creative: Chrissy Kwasnik
VP, Manufacturing: Alix Nicholaeff
VP, Group Managing Editor: Vicki Jaeger
Publishing Director: Mike Degler
Art Director: Catherine San Juan
Executive Editor: Jennifer Sims
Assistant Editors: Alex Figueiredo and Jeff Chiarelli
Managing Editor: Maria Spano
Senior Production Editor: Nora Milman
Production Associate: Deena Hashem
Senior Production Manager, Subsidiary Rights: Lina s Palma-Tenema

Insight Editions, in association with Roots of Peace, will plant two trees for each tree used in the manufacturing of this book. Roots of Peace is an internationally renowned humanitarian organization dedicated to eradicating land mines worldwide and converting war-torn lands into productive farms and wildlife habitats. Roots of Peace will plant two million fruit and nut trees in Afghanistan and provide farmers there with the skills and support necessary for sustainable land use.

Manufactured in China by Insight Editions

10 9 8 7 6 5 4 3 2 1